The White House and Education through the Years

Other Books by M. Scott Norton

The Principal as a Learning-Leader:
Motivating Students by Emphasizing Achievement

Competency-Based Leadership: A Guide for High
Performance in the Role of the School Principal

Teachers with the Magic: Great Teachers Change Students' Lives

The Changing Landscape of School Leadership:
Recalibrating the School Principalship

The Legal World of the School Principal:
What Leaders Need to Know about School Law

Guiding Curriculum Development:
The Need to Return to Local Control

Guiding the Human Resources Function in Education:
New Issues, New Needs

A Guide for Educational Policy Governance:
Effective Leadership for Policy Development

Dealing with Change: The Effects of Organizational
Development on Contemporary Practices

The White House and Education through the Years

U.S. Presidents' Views and Significant Education Contributions

M. Scott Norton

ROWMAN & LITTLEFIELD
Lanham • Boulder • New York • London

Published by Rowman & Littlefield
A wholly owned subsidiary of The Rowman & Littlefield Publishing Group, Inc.
4501 Forbes Boulevard, Suite 200, Lanham, Maryland 20706
www.rowman.com

Unit A, Whitacre Mews, 26–34 Stannary Street, London SE11 4AB

Copyright © 2018 by M. Scott Norton

All rights reserved. No part of this book may be reproduced in any form or by any electronic or mechanical means, including information storage and retrieval systems, without written permission from the publisher, except by a reviewer who may quote passages in a review.

British Library Cataloguing in Publication Information Available

Library of Congress Cataloging-in-Publication Data Available

ISBN 9781475840285 (cloth : alk. paper)
ISBN 9781475840292 (pbk. : alk. paper)
ISBN 9781475840308 (electronic)

∞™ The paper used in this publication meets the minimum requirements of American National Standard for Information Sciences—Permanence of Paper for Printed Library Materials, ANSI/NISO Z39.48–1992.

Printed in the United States of America

Contents

Preface   vii

Introduction   ix

1   Education Legacies of U.S. Presidents **1779–1829**:
The Era of Revolutionary America and the Young Republic   1

2   Education Views and Contributions of U.S. Presidents
1829–1877: The Era of War, Turmoil, and the New Nation   31

3   Education Legacies of U.S. Presidents **1877–1929**:
The Era of National Expansion, Reconstruction,
and the Second Industrial Revolution   53

4   Education Views and Contributions of U.S. Presidents
1929–1977: The Era of Depression, War, Postwar,
and the New Millennium   73

5   Education Legacies of U.S. Presidents **1977–2020**:
The New Millennium Era of Terrorism, Immigration,
and "Making America Great Again"   99

Appendix: Special Exercise   127

Glossary   131

About the Author   133

Preface
Why this Book was Written

The primary focus of the book is to provide information for administrators, teachers, students, and others relative to the important educational views and contributions of our forty-four U.S. presidents. What significant educational concepts on public education were pronounced by the nation's presidential leaders, and what far-reaching educational policies and practices were initiated during these presidents' administration? How have these personal views and legislative pronouncements influenced education at the time of their initiation and the future of education historically?

Attention is given to each president's thoughts and actions relative to the importance of education and how this importance is reflected in public statements of the president and in the actual educational practices/programs in America. What specific leadership is evidenced by the president that demonstrates his contributions to education in America? How have the pronouncements and governing leadership on education by presidents served to meet the important interests and needs of the children and youth of our nation over the years? How do the announced educational views of the nation's presidents correlate with their actual educational contributions?

There are differences in the educational accomplishments of the forty-four nation's presidential leaders. Each president has been faced with ongoing change, varying economic conditions, and an increasing diversity in the nation's citizenry. Depression, droughts, wars, immigration, technology, and other factors have placed major influences on the priorities of a president's agenda. As a new nation, early presidents were faced with a major concern for the success and retention of a democratic republic. What role was education to have in serving this purpose? History reveals that the large majority of our nation's presidents has viewed education as the essential factor for sustaining a democratic form of government. To what extent has this view been revealed in their legislative agendas?

The book considers each of the forty-four nation's presidents with respect to their expressed views on education in relation to its importance, its purposes, and policy/program developments during their administration. It is commonly known that the adopted U.S. Constitution does not mention the term "education." It always has been assumed that the Tenth Amendment to the Constitution leaves decisions about education to the various states. As the Tenth Amendment states, "Powers not granted to the United States were reserved to the states and its people." It has been generally believed that education was a federal concern, a state responsibility, and a local function.

Yet the involvement of the federal government over the years has been much more than a mere concern. Through the actions of Congress and pronouncements by national presidents, education has had much influence on public education. Federal programs related to vocational education, civil rights, church and state rulings, special needs education, curriculum requirements, physical fitness, funding, and other considerations are among the many interventions of education from the national level. How have the nation's presidents been active in the foregoing educational matters and others of paramount importance? The book focuses on the responses to these questions.

Introduction

How this Book is Organized

The eras in the development of our nation have been set forth in a number of published articles. However, we have selected five eras with respective dates for dividing the chapters of the book. For our purposes, we establish five major eras in the nation's development; each era serves as one chapter of the book. It is quite clear that eras tend to overlap rather than end in a certain year or even a decade. Each U.S. president, who served in the various eras, is discussed in the dominant era in which he served as president. For example:

Chapter 1 Era includes the presidents (colonial governance) who served during the years 1779 to 1829: the early years of the U.S. presidency.
Chapter 2 Era includes the presidents who served during the years 1829 to 1877: the American Revolution and the New Nation Era.
Chapter 3 Era includes the presidents who served during the years 1877 to 1929: national expansion and reconstruction period.
Chapter 4 Era includes the presidents who served during the years 1929 to 1977: postwar America and rise of industrial America to the Progressive Era.
Chapter 5 Era includes the presidents who served during the years 1977 to 2020: the new millennium, Clinton impeachment, Nixon resignation, nation's first black president, and "Making America Great Again."

Each chapter of the book opens with a statement of primary purpose. The specific presidents who served during the dates of the chapter coverage are discussed in relation to their expressed philosophy/beliefs related to the significance of public education. The identified policies, programs, and legislation considered and implemented during each president's tenure in office are reported. As is relevant to the chapter, some chapters have a pre-quiz to engage the readers and underscore important educational contributions. Quotations that demonstrate a president's educational beliefs are inserted. Specific educational quotations of the several presidents are underscored.

The book sets forth the early developments established by colonial leaders to place public education in the forefront of their new America. The ups and downs of the educational perspectives of the many national leaders demonstrate the important issues and problems that have faced and are facing the improvement of public education nationally. Although every effort is made to stay clear of the "politics" that is encountered in educational policy, its influence on educational matters such as control, funding, improvement, purpose, and availability is readily recognized in the views and contributions of the nation's presidential leaders. Although the book is not a history of a president's life or personal education—many books have been written on these topics—this book focuses on the educational views and personal contributions of the presidents to the maintenance and improvement of K–12 and higher education in America from the colonial period to the present time.

The book is written to be reader friendly with a look to the important history of educational beliefs and practices of public education in America. The contents of the book tend to identify the *educational presidents* who have served the nation over the years. Although persons in the various areas of public education will have a special interest in the history set forth in the book, persons in all other roles and occupations in America will be interested in the educational perspectives set forth by the nation's presidential leaders as well. As stated by President George Washington, "a primary objective should be the education of our youth and the sciences of government. In a republic, what species of knowledge can be equally important? And what more pressing than commuting it to those who are to be future guardians of our country?"

M. Scott Norton

Chapter 1

Education Legacies of U.S. Presidents 1779–1829

The Era of Revolutionary America and the Young Republic

Primary chapter goal: To underscore the importance of education in America as expressed in the views, contributions, and activities of the nation's presidential leaders during the early years of U.S. history.

Selected historical happenings that influenced this era: Boston Massacre; Boston Tea Party; First Continental Congress; American Revolution, Second Continental Congress; Paul Revere's Ride; War of Independence; Yorktown, Articles of Confederation; Revolution of 1800; Louisiana Purchase; Constitutional Convention; Lewis and Clark expedition; George Washington as America's first president; Jefferson; and the Declaration of Independence.

INTRODUCTION

In spite of the fact that the Constitution of the United States does not mention education and leaves the matter of education to the states and its people, the hand of the presidency historically has had significant influence on America's educational purposes and provisions. The Continental Congress was an assembly of delegates from the thirteen colonies, which became the governing body during the Revolutionary War. Such influences were embedded in the actions of the First Continental Congress as early as 1785 in its passage of the Land Ordinance of 1785 and later in the Northwest Land Ordinance of 1787 drafted by Thomas Jefferson. For example, the Land Ordinance of 1785 declared that the No. 16 lot of every township be reserved for the maintenance of public schools, which served as a significant thrust for public education and the future of the republic.

The land ordinance of 1785 focused on making public education a requirement within each township. All children were to be required to attend school. Not only did the colonists want all children to become good citizens but also there was a need to educate the young people for roles as ministers, priests, or capable office leaders. Besides setting each sixteenth section of the township for education, a section 19 was set for the purpose of religion and other arrangements for one or two universities. Compulsory public school attendance was well in mind, as was the concept of the separation of church and state.

Two years later, Congress approved the Land Ordinance of 1787. This legislation provided land that eventually became the five states of Michigan, Indiana, Wisconsin, Ohio, and Illinois. Article 3 of the ordinance stated that "religion, morality, and knowledge being necessary to good government and the happiness of mankind, schools and the means of education shall forever be encouraged" (League of Women Voters, 2011).

However, some schools did indeed teach religion along with reading and spelling and some sciences were integrated into a growing curriculum. It is noted that the "federal" government was mainly responsible for creating a public school for all children, and this model served well for expanding education in a growing territory toward the West.

Following the era of the colonization, settlement during the years 1620–1763, the eras of the American Revolution and the New Nation (1763–1825), the national expansion and reconstruction, the rise of industrial America, and the progressive Era were experienced in America. Thus, U.S. presidents Washington, J. Adams, Jefferson, Madison, Monroe, and J. Q. Adams each faced the problems of a growing, changing nation. This chapter centers on these eras with sole attention given to these presidents' views and contributions relative to public education.

We keep in mind that early U.S. presidents, as well as those in the middle and more recent years, had to face demanding national problems related to wars, depressions, militancy, foreign relationships, and other governance matters that dominated their time and energy. Public school matters were relegated, for the most part, to the individual states. From the earliest history of the seventeenth century, schools were being opened and education was indeed on the minds of the colonists. Many other individuals in the nation and within the states were giving much attention to public school education as well as the need for institutions of higher learning. For example, the Boston Latin School, the first public school, was founded in 1635. Four years later, the Mather School, the oldest public school in North America, was opened in Dorchester, Massachusetts.

Grammar schools were established in all the original thirteen colonies, and during the Reconstruction Era, public school systems were established that were supported by general taxes. Before 1900, many school programs were organized as one-room grade 1 through 8 schools. After 1900, high schools were established for the upper grades. Many of them were segregated schools. Later, some secondary schools were set up for black students. This practice became unlawful by the U.S. Supreme Court in 1954. Once again, the educational views and contributions of our nation's presidents are the focus here.

We only mention the foregoing educational history to emphasize the fact that education in the states continued to expand and improve over the years. The primary purpose of this book is not to present a history of education or to give primary attention to the education of the presidents themselves; that has been done in numerous publications. We focus on the objective of gaining an understanding of how the nation's early national leaders viewed the importance of education for sustaining the country's existence and assuring a happy life for members of the nation. As Washington noted, human happiness and moral duty are inseparably related. As of the time of this writing, there had been forty-four persons who had served in the presidency of the United States. However, we note that Donald Trump is considered to be the forty-fifth president since Grover Cleveland served as the twenty-second president and then again as the twenty-fourth president of the United States.

It must be kept in mind that the U.S. Constitution does not mention education, and the Tenth Amendment of the U.S. Constitution states that "the powers not delegated to the United States by the Constitution, nor prohibited by it to the States, are reserved to the States respectively, or to the people." Thus, establishing educational programs, policies, and financial support was not engraved in the minds of the early national leaders, even though its importance commonly was addressed in correspondence and public addresses. The business of establishing a new nation, dealing with Indian affairs, dealing with foreign relationships and wars, and resolving differences that were evident among the nation's early leaders dominated their interests and time.

We point out that special attention is given to the pronouncements and actual legislative actions that were taken by each president during his time in office. The information here and in later chapters is based, in large part, on statements set forth in the official papers and addresses of the U.S. presidents. Virtually all of this information evolves from the official governmental actions and papers that are viewed as being within the *public domain*, being available to the public as a whole, and therefore not subject to copyright. Many educational contributions of presidents took place before and after they were actually serving in the presidency. For that reason, before and after education–related activities are included in the discussion of their concepts and leadership activities.

Nevertheless, publications exemplified by Richardson's *Messages and Papers of the Presidents*, completed early in the late 1800s, serve as ready resources for the inaugural addresses, messages, papers, speeches, and statements by the early presidents of the United States.

According to one reference (Wikipedia, 2017, May 19), most presidents of the United States received a college education, even most of the earliest ones. Of the first seven presidents, five were college graduates. George Washington and Andrew Jackson did not have college degrees. Other presidents without college degrees include Lincoln, Van Buren, Taylor, Fillmore, A. Johnson, Cleveland, Monroe, Harrison, McKinley, and Truman. Of all the presidents, twenty-four of them graduated from private undergraduate colleges, nine graduated in a public undergraduate college, and twelve did not receive a degree. Every president since 1953 has held an undergraduate degree. President Woodrow Wilson is the only president who received a doctorate. Thus, close to one-third of the nation's presidents had not earned college degrees.

George Washington, John Adams, Thomas Jefferson, James Madison, and James Monroe, all members of the Continental Congress, established by the first thirteen colonies as a governing body during the Revolutionary War, later served as presidents of the United States. In this chapter, the educational views and achievements of U.S. presidents who served from 1779 to 1829 are discussed. Presidents who served through the years 1829–1877, 1877–1929, 1929–1977, and 1977–2020 are discussed later in chapters 2, 3, 4, and 5, respectively.

A SPECIAL NOTE

It was noted in the preface of the book that the central focus of the book is to report on the personal views and contributions of presidents of the United States relative to public education in America. Thus, we purposely avoid reporting on the life history of the U.S. presidents; the history and biographical sketches of the presidents have been reported many times in books, articles, and other publications over the years. There is one exception in this regard. We set forth a brief "photo" of selected historical events and personalities at the outset of each chapter in order to amplify the conditions, issues, and status of the times. In addition, toward the end of each chapter, we report on one related historical happening or interesting story that occurred in each of the five eras.

These brief happenings/stories are intended to make the book more reader friendly and often center on a completely new "learning" for the reader. The event is not related directly to education, but does give the reader an additional view of the era under discussion. We title these added briefs "Selected Event of Interest during This Era."

Once again, we note that the book's focus is on the views that our presidents have voiced on the importance of universal education in America and to report on the important contributions of each president in relation to legislation proposed or passed, proclamations on education set forth, and presidential rulings that were made during the time of serving in the office of president, and the time before and after serving as president. We begin by presenting the education legacy of the nation's first president, George Washington.

GEORGE WASHINGTON
THE COLONIZATION ERA

George Washington (1789–1797)

We begin with George Washington, the first U.S. president, who served eight years in the presidency from 1789 to 1797. George Washington's beliefs relative to the importance of education and the future of the country were expressed in personal quotes such as the following:

> A primary objective should be the education of our youth and the sciences of government. In a republic, what species of knowledge can be equally important?
>
> And what is more pressing than commuting it to those who are to be future guardians of our country?
>
> Nor am I less persuaded, that you will agree with me in opinion that there is nothing which can better deserve our patronage than the promotion of science and literature. Knowledge is in every country the surest basis of public happiness.
>
> The more homogeneous our Citizens can be made in these particulars, the greater will be our prospect of permanent union; and primary object of such a national Institution should be the education of our youth in the science of *government*. In a republic what species of knowledge can be equally important and what duty more pressing on its legislature than to patronize a plan for communicating it to those who are to be the future guardians of the liberties of the country?

Washington on the Importance of Educating the Nation's Young People

Cook and Klay (2014) expertly set forth the visions of George Washington relative to his thinking about educating future citizens of the new nation. We give credit to these two professional educators for the following summary of Washington's thoughts on education. Washington's interest in promoting education for young persons included the focus of national community with emphasis on educating young persons in America as opposed to studying in universities outside America. He contended that learning the science of government would best be achieved by studying the topic of governance locally; the nation's economic prosperity and effective leadership would benefit as a result.

Washington considered the topics of history, foreign languages, mathematics, moral behavior, and the science of government as being of special importance. As previously noted, he believed that the right education of youth was the best means for fostering a strong and happy citizenry. In addition, a quality education would do much to resolve the problems of illiteracy and poverty that served to undermine the foundation of a democratic society. His views of a *liberal education* would be important in fostering a sense of social responsibility and the factors that served to provide the knowledge and skills required in contributing to a successful life in the real world. A *liberal education* is generally defined as being based on the liberal arts and intended to bring about the improvement, discipline, or free development of the mind or spirit.

Washington's empathy for children with special needs was revealed by his personal financial donations for educating children who were orphans and other children whose parents did not have the means to support their schooling. According to a letter sent to Thomas Jefferson (1785), Washington expressed the desire to help children of soldiers who were killed in the Revolutionary War. His ideas of universal education were to serve the purpose of assuring an educated citizenry, one that was vital for supporting and maintaining a democratic nation.

Washington's Leadership toward Promoting Institutions of Higher Learning

Washington believed that institutions of higher learning could serve the nation in various ways. The nation's youth could be educated in the many aspects of government, the arts and sciences could be emphasized, public administration leadership could be fostered, and liberal studies could facilitate the importance of participative citizenship for supporting the values of a successful republic. Socialization was of paramount importance for bringing about a cooperative attitude and the ability to interact for the purpose of defeating separatism and prejudices. Effective policy development depended on such conditions.

Although Washington did not have a college degree, his concepts and personal behaviors revealed his competence and understanding of the complexities of public policy, including financial matters, the science of government, managerial ability, economics, the implications of enlightenment, and the importance of promoting the values of citizenship and public service through a program of liberal education. He envisioned an education system that emphasized the liberal studies and processes of socializing to enhance a sense of national community by giving student an education in the science of government (Cook and Klay, 2014).

Washington's Early Promotion of Higher Education

As specifically stated by Washington in his Eighth Annual Address to the Senate and House of Representatives on December 7, 1796:

> I have heretofore proposed to the Consideration of Congress the expediency of Congress of establishing a national university and also a military academy. The desirableness of both of these institutions has so constantly increased with every new view I have taken of the subject that I cannot omit the opportunity of once and for all recalling your attention to them.

> The assembly to which I address myself is too enlightened not to be full sensible how much a flourishing state of the arts and sciences contributes to national prosperity and reputation. . . . Amongst the motives to such an institution, the assimilation of the principles, opinions, and manners of our countrymen by the common education of a portion of our youth from every quarter well deserves attention. The more homogeneous our citizens can be made in these particulars the greater will be our prospect of permanent union; and a primary object of such a national institution should be the education of our youth to the science of government.

Washington's Farewell Address on September 17, 1796, began by addressing Friends and Fellow-Citizens. Later, in the address, he stated that "it is substantially true that virtue or morality is a necessary spring of popular government. The rule indeed extends with more or less force to every species of free government. Who that is a sincere friend to it can look with indifference upon attempts to shake the foundations of the fabric? Promote, then, as an object of primary importance, institutions for the general diffusion of knowledge. In proportion as the structure of a government gives force to public opinion, it is essential that public opinion should be enlightened." Washington was well aware that an educated citizenry would be more appreciative of the fact that taxation for educational purposes was necessary to support the efficient functioning of a democratic government.

Cook and Klay (2014) underscored the fact that George Washington was adamant about establishing a plan of universal education in the United States. Washington argued that an educated citizenry was essential for able participation in a democratic government. This belief was expressed later by Thomas Jefferson and other national leaders. Washington's concept of an educated citizenry and a viable democracy was indeed one of his most important recommendations for determining contemporary purposes of elementary and secondary education in our nation. "Washington sought to promote Enlightenment-based ideas to guide the education of young people. He reasoned that citizens who have learned to think for themselves would strive to perpetuate the republic" (Cook and Klay, 2014, 63).

Washington was one of the very first national leaders to conceive of an educational program for children that gave them the essential capacity to be individual thinkers and follow up with liberal studies that that gave youth and older learners a broaden understanding and knowledge that was necessary for future leadership to sustain a democratic republic (Cook and Klay, 2014). His concept of early education for children and youth was somewhat parallel to contemporary elementary and secondary school organization.

Washington's Education Legacy in Summary

George Washington's influence on education in America began even before he was elected to the position of president of the United States in 1789. As a member of the Continental Congress, he was instrumental in passing legislation that established the Land Ordinance of 1785 that declared that lot No. 16 of every township be reserved for the maintenance of public schools. Washington's tireless attention to establishing a national system of enlightenment served as a foundation for giving each student the knowledge and skills needed for knowledgeable participation and leadership in a democratic republic. He presided over the 1787 Convention that drafted the U.S. Constitution and ultimately became known as the father of the country.

From the very outset of his presidency, Washington was unrelenting in his efforts to promote an enlightened educational program for all children and youth. The future of the American system of freedom and happiness depended on an educated citizenry. *Enlightenment* centered on an intellectual movement, which dominated the world of ideas during the seventeenth and eighteenth centuries.

In his First Annual Address to the Senate and House of Representatives in 1790, President Washington stated quite clearly his views on the vital importance of knowledge as promoted by science and literature that were the basic surest basis of public happiness. Keep in mind that the following words were expressed by Washington early in the history of the nation. An organized school program was yet to be established in the various states. The Civil War was seventy-one years in the future. No organized teacher preparation programs existed in the nation. The first two-year normal school in the nation for teacher training did not open in Concord, Vermont, for another thirty-three years. As Washington stated:

> Nor am I less persuaded that you will agree with me in opinion that there is nothing which can better deserve your patronage than the promotion of science and literature.
>
> Knowledge is in every country the surest basis of public happiness. . . . To the security of a free constitution it contributes in various ways—by convincing those who are entrusted with the public administration that every valuable end of government is best answered by the enlightened confidence of the people, and by teaching the people themselves to know and to value their own rights; to discern and provide against invasions of them; to distinguish between oppression and necessary exercise of lawful authority; between burthens proceeding from that of licentiousness—cherishing the first, avoiding the last—and uniting a speedy but temperate vigilance against encroachments, with an inviolable respect to the laws.

Washington often spoke of the two dimensions of education, one for young students for the purpose of helping them to think wisely for themselves and gain a liberal education for gaining the knowledge needed for participating as a knowledgeable citizen in the American society. A second dimension centered on higher education, which could provide specialized training in a variety of areas, including preparation for leadership of paramount importance for sustaining a democratic republic.

Washington's views and messages to others stressed the importance of a liberal education. Of special interest were Washington's specifications in his will that his slaves be freed and given an opportunity to learn to read and write.

JOHN ADAMS

John Adams (1797–1801)

John Adams, the second president of the United States, was clear in setting forth his primary views on the importance of a free public education for all the people. The citizenry of the United States, whether having school-age children or not, was benefactors of an educated citizenry. Thus, public financial support of education was a legitimate public expenditure. Adams, like George Washington and other national presidents to follow, viewed an educated citizenry as essential for the maintenance of a democratic republic. As he contended, "Liberty cannot be preserved without general knowledge among the people." In addition, he noted that the end of study is to make one a good man and a useful citizen.

Education for all served as a primary theme for Adams' beliefs on public education; great accomplishments for the nation depended on it. Free, public education must include what Adams termed the lower ranks of society as well. Schools and institutions of higher education should not be confined to a few; rather it must become the national concern and the financial support for the education of the American citizenry.

Specifically, Adams stated that "the education here intended is not merely of the children of the rich and noble, but of every rank and class of people, down to the lowest and the poorest. It is not too much to say that schools for the education of all should be placed at convenient distances, and maintained at the public expense." Adams viewed the laws for the liberal education for the lower classes of people to be especially wise and useful. In his view, no expense for this purpose would be thought extravagant. Adams' contentions were demonstrated additionally in the following quotations:

> But before any great things are accomplished, a memorable change must be made in the system of Education and knowledge must become so general as to raise the lower ranks of Society nearer to the higher. The Education of a Nation, instead of being confined to a few schools & Universities, for the instruction of a few, must become the National Care and experience, for the information of the Many.
>
> Liberty cannot be preserved without a general knowledge among the people who have a right from the frame of their nature to knowledge, as their great Creator who does nothing in vain, has given them understanding and desire to know. But besides this they have a right, an indisputable, unalienable, indefeasible divine right to the more dreaded and envied kind of knowledge, I mean the characters and conduct of their rulers. You will ever remember that all the end of study is to make you a good man and a useful citizen.
>
> Children should be instructed in the principles of freedom.
>
> Liberty cannot be preserved without general knowledge among the people.
>
> The whole people must take it upon themselves the education of the whole people and be willing to bear the expenses of it. There should not be a district of one mile square, without a school in it, not founded by a charitable individual, but maintained at the public expense of the people themselves.

Adams was adamant in his promotion of education for all citizens, even though some persons contend that he was referring to Caucasians rather than black people. We believe differently. The following Adams' contention is clear in giving the opportunities and advantages of education to different orders of the people and in all parts of the country with emphasis on literature and the sciences. He believed that the happiness of the people was the sole end of government and the consent of the people was foundational to its success.

As previously contended by Washington, and later by Jefferson, Adams felt strongly that liberty could not be sustained without a knowledgeable citizenry. People have a right, along with an unquestionable divine right, to have knowledge concerning the characters and behaviors of their rulers.

Thus, liberty could not be preserved without the general knowledge of all the citizenry. But, to accomplish this end, educational practices must be changed and knowledge must become so general that it reaches all ranks of society. School and universities must become instruction for the many.

It is interesting to note John Adams' perspective on reading. He noted that he just could not satisfy his passion for reading. He stated that the more one reads the more one sees that we have to read. "Let us dare to read, think, and write," he once proclaimed. At one time, Adams said, "I must judge for myself, but how can I judge, how can any man judge, unless his mind has opened and enlarged by reading." As a side note, we point out that John Adams was one of the thirteen vice-presidents who also ultimately served as president of the United States.

Although John Adams had many accomplishments while in office as the second president of the United States, his actual accomplishments for public education are rarely mentioned, if at all, in his biographical history. Certainly, Adams was a hard worker while in office, having sat on no less than ninety committees along with his primary duties as the nation's president. Adams' basic ideas and principles were included in the final version of the U.S. Constitution even though education was never mentioned in that historic document. Nevertheless, many court cases involving educational matters and the freedoms and rights of faculty and students in educational settings were determined on the basis of constitutional law.

Diplomatic accomplishments for John Adams while in office as president were of paramount importance to America's future. His educational quotations are quite specific regarding his views on education. The responsibility for financial educational support for all citizens by the general public was quite clear in Adams' thinking. Missing is the specific evidence of Adams' actions, policies, and leadership on educational matters during his administration from 1797 to 1801. It is true that the development of education was in its infancy at the time of Adams' administration. Important educational developments took place during the next eight years under the presidency of Thomas Jefferson.

In a review of John Adams' papers and proclamations was one proclamation (March 6, 1799) for Thanksgiving suggested by Adams as a day of solemn humiliation, fasting, and prayer. The day recommended for the observance was Thursday, the twenty-fifth day of April. Among all of the suggested benefits of the day would be the Supreme Beings smile on the colleges, academies, schools, and seminaries of learning, and make them nurseries of sound science, morals, and religion. Once again, the statements on education and its importance are spread throughout Adams' writings, but the evidence of policy development, program recommendations, and other educational activities on his part are missing from his history and presidential accomplishments.

THOMAS JEFFERSON

Thomas Jefferson (1801-1809)

Thomas Jefferson, president of the United States from 1801 to 1809, is well known for his significant contributions to America's Constitution, but he was a man of many talents and his influence on education benefited from them. We focus primarily on his contributions to education during his years in the president's office, although he made positive contributions before and after he completed his eight years in the president's office.

Enlightenment was a movement during the eighteenth century that dominated the world's thinking with an emphasis on rationalism as opposed to the traditional and political ideas that dominated traditional thinking. Thus, it was also known as the age of reason. Enlightenment was underscored by the belief that science and logical reasoning gave the individual the opportunity to gain more knowledge and understanding than traditional practices. Man's mind was capable of gaining knowledge and understanding through thoughtful actions and using scientific methodology.

Civic literacy was needed by all citizens of the republic to protect their human liberties and personal rights. As a member of the state of Virginia's state legislature, Jefferson introduced bills, which centered on the diffusion of knowledge for all citizens, amending the charter of William and Mary to remove theological control from the curriculum and to establish a public library in Richmond, Virginia (Gutek, 1986).

A Bill for the More General Diffusion of Knowledge set forth an education plan for the State of Virginia. Each county was to be divided into small districts of five to six square miles for a school that focused on the teaching of the three r's, reading, writing, and arithmetic. Teachers for each school were to be supported by those persons who sent their child to the school free for the first three years and then paying for the school after that time. Top students of parents who were unable to pay for additional education were supported for further education in higher schools for instruction in languages, geography, and higher levels of arithmetic. Best students in this category were eligible for further learning for an additional six years.

Many students who graduated from the grammar schools became teachers themselves or were given monetary support to attend the College of William & Mary. However, Jefferson's bill did not pass the Virginia Assembly, but later a lesser plan for public education was instituted in 1796. Jefferson's basic plan for organizing public education was continued by other well-known public school leaders such as Horace Mann, Benjamin Rush, Noah Webster, Samuel Knox, Robert Coram, and Harrison Smith. Jefferson's support of a program for the diffusion of knowledge was supported in his letters to George Washington and John Adams.

In a letter to Washington, in 1786, Jefferson expressed the belief that the liberties of the people necessitated their being in the hands of an educated citizenry. In a letter to John Adams in 1813, Jefferson was hopeful that public schools would become the keystone in the arch of our government. Jefferson did not favor education being controlled by state or federal agencies. That is, the local school district and its parents were best suited to control the common school. Specifically, he was of the opinion that education could not be effective by any authority other than the parents of each ward. Decentralization was the central focus of Jefferson's plan for public schools. Any centralized control by the state was objectionable in the view of Jefferson.

Jefferson held the belief that the parents in the school district could pay for most of the required educational expenses. Children of poor parents who were unable to pay would attend the school free. Small county taxes could cover the minimal additional school fees. History has shown that Jefferson's belief in this respect was faulty, although a teacher's salary was indeed minimal in those times; most teachers were talented persons, while many were just graduates of high school programs. In any case, Jefferson questioned placing the governance of schools under government control. Nevertheless, he was somewhat inconsistent regarding the governance question. His statements tended to change from parental control to dividing it among the various entities in relation to their respective competencies.

Another interesting educational consideration was that of compulsory attendance. For various reasons, many parents did not want their child to attend a common school. One reason centered on the fact was that a child's help was needed at home. In addition, a major concern was that of the child's influences outside the home and church. Home schooling and teachings of the church placed more control on what was to be implemented in the minds of the young children. Would outside teaching give the child ideas outside the will of the parents? It is true that parents did want their child to be able to read for this skill as it was necessary for being able to read the Bible.

Representative educational views of Jefferson are noted in his following quotes:

> Every government degenerates when trusted to the rulers of the people. The people themselves, therefore, are its only safe depositories. And to render them safe, their minds must be improved to a certain degree. (Notes on Virginia Q.XIV, 1782. ME 2:207)

> Though (the people) may acquiesce, they cannot approve what they do not understand. (Appointment Bill, 1792, ME 3.211)

> If the Wise be the happy man . . . he must be virtuous too; for without virtue, happiness cannot be. This then is the true scope of all academical emulation. (To Samuel Knox, 1810, ME 12:360)

> If the condition of man is to be progressively ameliorated, as we fondly hope and believe, education is to be the chief instrument in effecting it. (To A. Julien, 1818, ME 15:172)

> Above all things I hope the education of the common people will be attended to, convinced that on their good sense we may rely with the most security for the preservation of a due degree of liberty. (To James Madison, 1787, FE 4:480)

The contention that freedom and democracy were privileges bestowed by royalty or other monarchs was faulty. *Enlightenment* viewed freedom and democracy as fundamental human rights. Enlightenment was to be dependent on the education of the public by means of education. Education was for all the citizenry, not just royalty and the well to do. Reading was of paramount importance for all the people. Literacy was necessary for gaining a literate public; reading was essential for young people in order for them to be able to read the Bible. *Egalitarianism* was prominent in the minds of the public; freedom and democracy was a fundamental right of all the people. Egalitarianism is the doctrine that people are equal with respect to social, political, and economic affairs.

Besides Thomas Jefferson, other prominent persons who were leaders of the Enlightenment Era included Benjamin Franklin, John Locke, Sir Isaac Newton, Thomas Pain, Voltaire, and others.

Jefferson's Education Pronouncements in Letters and Presidential Actions

Jefferson's most frequently cited quote on education, "If a nation expects to be ignorant and free, in a state of civilization, it expects what never was or never will be," was stated in a letter to Charles Yancey, seven years after his presidential term. Yet, his untiring efforts to gain universal education opportunities for all citizens was set forth in a reply to the American Philosophical Society in 1808 as follows: "I feel . . . an ardent desire to see knowledge so disseminated through the mass of mankind that it may, at length, reach even the extremes of society: beggars and kings."

Segarra (2013) of the *Daily Signal*, points out several views of Jefferson on educational reform. She notes Jefferson's view of basic education for bringing about "life, liberty, and pursuit of happiness" for all Americans. With a basic education in hand, a child could become capable for self-expression and improve his or her morals and faculties with the ability to read efficiently. In addition, citizens would be able to be proficient in understanding their rights, be able to judge the matters of voting, and recognize government's infringements on their liberties. The end result is witnessed in the ability of each individual to develop his or her own happiness in life; good health, occupation, and freedom of just pursuits would result.

Jefferson spoke of elementary schools that would be served best if managed by parents within community wards. This arrangement would place the educational care of each child under the care of persons who cared the most, the parents. That is, parents were viewed by Jefferson as being the best managers of a child's education. Empowering parents over their child's education and the dollars being spent on it would result in the improvement of educational outcomes. As stated by Jefferson in a letter to Jarvis (Foley,

1900), "I know of no safe depository of the ultimate powers of the society but the people themselves; but if we think them not enlightened enough to exercise their control with a wholesome discretion, the remedy is not to take it from them, but to inform their discretion by education."

Jefferson was one president who took great interest in public schools after leaving office. He wrote in a letter to John Adams several years after leaving the presidency that he was in hope that the public schools would come to be the keystone in the arch of our government. However, Jefferson did not favor state government's control over the district schools. To do so, in his mind, would result in mismanagement and questionable financial expenditures. In Jefferson's opinion, state control of public education would end in mismanagement and divorced from the supervision of the child's parents. In addition, a government could no more manage schools than manage farms, mills, or local businesses.

Jefferson's legislative bill on education in Virginia stipulated that free public schools be established every five to six square miles. Specifically, as proposed by Jefferson in one bill: "This proposed to divide every county into wards of 5. or 6. miles square, like your townships; to establish in each ward a free school for reading, writing and common arithmetic; to provide for annual selection of the best subjects from these schools who might receive the public expense of a higher degree of education at a district from these district schools to select a certain number of the most promising subjects to be completed (*sic*) at an University, where all the useful sciences should be taught."

Thus, the concept of a neighborhood school was to be implemented. Jefferson's neighborhood school concept swept into many other states and school districts later until the early 1930s. In the years that followed, school district reorganization became the cry for reducing the number of school boards, increasing the size of school districts, supposedly decreasing educational expenditures, and thus reducing public taxes. Jefferson courageously tackled many of the educational problems and needs facing the nation including the common school program, diversity, needy children, special needs students, and an educational system from the early grades to higher education.

Jefferson's early interest in higher education was demonstrated by his actions in 1779 to revise the curriculum of the College of William & Mary and his early plans for initiating a new university in Virginia. As the elected Governor of Virginia, he also served on the board of visitors of the College of William & Mary. In 1800, one year previous to his election to the presidency, Jefferson sent a letter to a leading Virginia politician setting forth his interest in establishing a liberal and modern university in the state of Virginia. Seventeen years later, the cornerstone for the first building of what was to be the University of Virginia was placed on a plot of land just west of Charlottesville, Virginia (Zechmeister, 2011).

Government matters such as Indian affairs, foreign relations including various treaties, military affairs, the Louisiana Purchase, boundary settlements, and the myriad of other executive matters consumed the attention of President Jefferson. As a result, he had little real success implementing his ideas relative to universal education. Without question, many of Jefferson's ideas of education for all citizens, special consideration for special needs of children and youth, and full attention to services for children of lower-income families are in place in most public schools today. In addition, many of Jefferson's contributions to education were realized following his term as president.

Nine years after leaving the Executive Office of President of the United States, in a letter to Joseph Cabell, Jefferson wrote that "a system of general instruction, which shall reach every description of our citizens from the richest to the poorest, as it was the earliest, so will it be the latest of all public concerns in which I shall permit myself to take an interest." One evidence of this continued interest was Jefferson's establishment of the University of Virginia. This achievement set the stage for a national education system and a planned system for education at the public school level.

Jefferson's Founding of the University of Virginia

Besides being well known for his efforts for establishing the U.S. Constitution and the writing of the Declaration of Independence, Jefferson's longtime efforts to establish the University of Virginia in Charlottesville, Virginia, are among his most memorable education accomplishments. It was not until 1825, sixteen years after he left the presidency, that the university opened its doors to only five foreign professors and a few dozen students (Zechmeister, 2011). According to Zechmeister, two more professors and more than 100 students were in attendance by the end of the first year. Jefferson's early vision of a future university viewed it as not being a house but an academical village.

Jefferson last visited the University of Virginia in early June 1826. The father of the University of Virginia died soon thereafter on July 4, 1826.

JAMES MADISON

The demands of the office of president were such that Madison had little time to give attention to the national matters of public education. As stated in his first inaugural address, "The present situation of the world is indeed without a parallel, and that of our own country full of difficulties." The matters of raising additional military forces, the belligerency of the British

James Madison (1809–1817)

Government and France, reorganization of the military, Indian affairs and treaties, army desertions, and war were just a few of the difficulties faced by Madison's presidency. However, Madison's views on the importance of education were expressed by him during, before, and after his term of president. Representative educational quotes of Madison are set forth in the following section.

Note that the themes of having a public education with the "haves" paying for the education of the "have nots," the close relationship of liberty being based on learning, knowledge being necessary for an effective government, the need for parents to aid in supporting their child's education financially, and the overriding concept of having a public-funded education are emphasized throughout Madison's educational beliefs emphasized in the following statements:

> Learned Institutions ought to be the favorite objects with every free people. They throw that light over the public mind which is the best security against crafty and dangerous encroachments on the public liberty.

> The liberal appropriations made by the Legislature of Kentucky for a general system of Education cannot be too much applauded. A popular Government, without popular information, or the means of acquiring it, is but a Prologue to a Farce or a Tragedy, or, perhaps both. Knowledge will forever govern ignorance. And a people who mean to be their own Governors, must arm themselves with the power which knowledge gives.

> A *popular government* is one that is controlled by the people by election and subject to the will of the popular sovereignty.

> Its rapid growth & signal prosperity in this character have afforded me much pleasure; which is not a little enhanced by the enlightened patriotism which is now provided for the State a Plan of Education embracing every class of Citizens, and every grade and department of Knowledge. No error is more certain

than the one proceeding from a hasty & superficial view of the subject: that the people at large have no interest in the establishment of Academies, Colleges, and Universities, where a few only, and those not of the poorer classes can obtain their sons the advantages of superior education. It is thought to be unjust that all should be taxed for the benefit of a part, and that to the part least needing it.

At cheaper and nearer seats of Learning parents with slender incomes may place their sons in a course of education putting them on the level with the sons of the Richest. Whilst those who are without property, or with but little, must be peculiarly interested in a System which unites with the more Learned Institutions, a provision for diffusing through the entire Society the education needed for the common purposes of life (emphasis added).

In the foregoing quotations, one might view such terms as the "sons of the richest," "those poorer classes can obtain their *sons* the advantage," and "may place their *sons* in a course of education" as biased in relation to the rights of daughters. Some authorities have suggested that the statements of our early national leaders are indeed directed toward the male citizenry alone. Madison was of the opinion that when a youth merited an education and his or her parents could not afford to support his education, he or she should be carried forward at public expense.

We choose not to accept the foregoing contention, although one must keep in mind that voting rights for female citizens were not sanctioned until 1920. The many early statements for the need of an educated citizenry lead toward the belief that all citizens were considered in relation to the important future of the nation.

At the time the United States was founded, however, female citizens did not have the same rights as male members, including voting rights. The right for women to vote did not occur until August 18, 1920, when the Nineteenth Amendment to the Constitution gave American women the right to vote known as *women suffrage*. This legislative action was not taken until more than 100 years after Madison left the office of president. Nevertheless, Madison, as well as all previous presidents, was a strong supporter of public education. This fact is revealed in his thoughts about government and its dependence on knowledge and the power that it gives to leadership:

A popular government without popular information or the means of acquiring it is both a prologue to a farce or a tragedy, or perhaps, both. Knowledge will forever govern ignorance; and a people who mean to be their own governors must arm themselves with the power which knowledge gives.

An interesting side note regarding Madison's contributions to America's future was noted by Stagg (2017). Stagg wrote that, by September 1787, Madison had emerged from the Constitutional Convention as the most impressive and persuasive voice in favor of a new constitution, eventually earning the title "Father of the Constitution," a title most often attributed to

Thomas Jefferson. In addition, and of great importance, Madison introduced and guided to passage the first ten amendments to the Constitution. These amendments, known as the Bill of Rights, have served the rights of all citizens including teachers and students in public education historically.

JAMES MONROE

James Monroe (1817–1825)

Although little evidence is found regarding educational policies and/or programs initiated by James Monroe, it is quite clear that he viewed the promotion of intelligence among the people as the best means of preserving the citizens' liberties. In his First Inaugural Address, Monroe stated that

> it is only when the people become ignorant and corrupt, when they degenerate into a populace, that they are incapable of exercising the sovereignty. Usurpation is then an easy attainment, and a usurper soon found. The people themselves become the willing instruments of their own debasement and ruin. Let us then, to the great cause, and endeavor to preserve it in full force. Let us by all wise and constitutional measures promote intelligence among the people as the best means of preserving our liberties.

There is no question that Madison was a supporter of public education and, in fact, he supported the assessment of property taxes to pay for it.

The Right of Congress to Establish Institutions for the Diffusion of Knowledge

It is commonly known that the U.S. Constitution did not include the topic of education and that the Tenth Amendment of the Constitution gave the rights on matters, not given to the United States, to the states and/or its people. It is quite clear, however, that education might have been overlooked by the drafters of the Constitution. Some evidence of the feeling of such an oversight was addressed by Monroe in his First Inaugural Address presented to Congress on April 15, 1815.

When speaking of the advantages of having such facilities as roads and canals, Monroe questioned the right of Congress to initiate such improvements but recommended that an amendment be approved to assure that right. In seeking such an amendment, Monroe recommended that it include the right to institute seminaries of learning for the all-important purpose of diffusing knowledge among fellow-citizens throughout the United States. Later in history, Article 1, Section 8, of the U.S. Constitution was used to justify the intervention of Congress into various educational programs.

Article 1, Section 8, states that "the Congress shall have the power to lay and collect taxes . . . and provide for the Common Defence and general Welfare of the United States." Thus, the power to provide for the common defense and *general welfare* of the citizenry has been used over the years to justify Congress' involvement, intervention, and control of various state and local school district educational matters. Such controls have advanced over the years. Nevertheless, all during the eight years of Monroe's presidency, the matter of the federal government's power and jurisdiction over various matters of the states was in question.

It is difficult to discuss any topic relative to the life of James Madison without mentioning one of the most important foreign policy documents in the history of the United States, the Monroe Doctrine. The law established the future of colonization in Latin America by the Spanish and the European nations. Monroe objected to such expansion. As set forth in the doctrine, further efforts by European nations to colonize land or interfere with states in North or South America would be considered as acts of aggression and, thus, would require the intervention of the United States.

In addition, Monroe assisted in negotiations for the purchase of the Louisiana Territory, the purchase of Florida from Spain (supported the Treaty of 1818 with Great Britain, which allowed settlers into the Pacific Northwest) and other actions that served the nation's ability to preserve its territory and open it for national purposes, including education.

When his presidency ended on March 4, 1824, Monroe resided at Monroe Hill, what is now included in the grounds of the University of Virginia. He had operated a family farm from 1788 to 1817 but sold it in the first year of his presidency to the new university. He served on the board of visitors under Jefferson and under Rector James Madison until his death on July 4, 1831.

JOHN QUINCY ADAMS

John Quincy Adams (1825–1829)

John Quincy Adams served one four-year term as president of the United States from 1825 to 1829. Although he viewed the acquisition of knowledge as being of paramount importance, his administrative record revealed limited accomplishments in that direction. Nevertheless, he believed that to furnish the means of acquiring knowledge was the greatest benefit that could be conferred upon mankind; it prolongs life itself and enlarges the sphere of existence. Yet Adams' personal contributions to public education in America were few.

In John Q. Adams' First Inaugural Address in 1825, while addressing how our country could improve, he underscored the importance of education as related to the enjoyments of human life. He viewed knowledge as being among the first, perhaps the very first, instrument for the improvement of the condition of men and for the acquisition of much of the knowledge to the wants, comforts, and enjoyment of human life. Therefore, in the mind of Adams, public institutions and seminaries of learning were essential.

Later in his inaugural address, he pointed to the year now ending and praised the work of one state for its approval and funding of a new university that had unfolded its portals to the sons of science and upheld the torch of human improvement for all to see. We keep in mind, at this early time in the nation's history, that education was viewed as a state responsibility. Nationally, Indian affairs, troublesome foreign relationships, and internal territory decisions, along with efforts for approving new states and expanding territories, took the lion's share of John Q. Adams' time and energy.

POST-CHAPTER QUIZ

Multiple Choice

Directions: For each of the following ten multiple choice questions, circle the correct response.

1. An early and significant action of the Continental Congress concerning the establishment of education nationally was the approval of:

   a The Land Ordinance of 1785.
   b The Louisiana Purchase in 1803.
   c Johns Quincy Adams' signing of the Monroe Doctrine.
   d The passing of legislation that gave women the right to vote.

2. In expressing the vital importance of education, the large majority of the nation's early presidents underscored:

   a Its rights for all citizens of the United States.
   b Its importance for preparing leaders for the nation's economic future.
   c Its vital importance for assuring an educated citizenry and sustaining a democratic government and personal freedom.
   d Its vital importance for training young men for military leadership and defense of the nation against all enemies whomsoever.

3. An intellectual and philosophical movement that dominated the world of ideas in Europe and many of the early leaders of the nation placed an emphasis on:

   a Rationalism versus traditional political ideas.

b Enlightenment of the public through education.
c The scientific method.
d Having knowledge or understanding of the act of giving someone knowledge.
e None of the above.
f All of the above.

4. In which year did Congress pass the Nineteenth Amendment to the U.S. Constitution, which gave women the right to vote?

   a 1800
   b 1850
   c 1900
   d 1920
   e None of the above

5. When it came to the control of the elementary and secondary schools in the states, Jefferson favored that the control be in the hands of:

   a The federal government.
   b State governors and state officials.
   c The parents of each school ward.
   d Any federal or state department such as the agricultural and social welfare departments.

6. Which president of the United States in his Eighth Annual Address set forth the following educational statement? "I have heretofore proposed to the consideration of Congress, the expediency of establishing a National University; and also a Military Academy."

   a George Washington
   b John Adams
   c Thomas Jefferson
   d James Monroe
   e John Quincy Adams
   f None of the above

7. Which early president openly expressed his passion for reading? In doing so, he said, "Let us dare to read, think and write."

   a John Adams
   b Thomas Jefferson
   c James Madison
   d James Monroe
   e John Quincy Adams

8. Which reason or reasons below most likely influenced the slow movement of public education in early America?

   a The fact that education was not mentioned in the U.S. Constitution.
   b The fact that responsibilities not reserved for the United States in the Constitution were delegated to the states.
   c The fact that territories and states within the growing boundaries of the country were not completely settled and new states were being added from time to time.
   d Early national presidents had to give most of their attention to matters of foreign policy, Indian affairs, wars, territorial matters including new states and boundaries, sustaining the republic, and other national governance matters.
   e All of the above.

9. Which of the early presidents of the United States gave the most direct consideration to the development of elementary, secondary, and higher education in the United States during his lifetime?

   a George Washington
   b John Adams
   c Thomas Jefferson
   d James Madison
   e James Monroe
   f John Quincy Adams

10. What significance, if any, does the following entry in the U.S. Constitution hold for the federal government and public education? The entry: "The Congress shall have the power to lay and collect taxes . . . and provide for the common defense and general welfare of the United States."

    a The statement holds no significance for educational involvement in public education.
    b The statement gives Congress additional support for collecting educational taxes.
    c The statement gives Congress a free hand in public school governance.
    d The statement "provide for the common defense and general welfare of the United States" has been interpreted to mean that the federal government can intervene in education when the general welfare of the country is at stake.

True or False

1. The importance of education for the successful future of the new America was clearly set forth in the U.S. Constitution. ____True or False____

2. Neither George Washington nor Abraham Lincoln, although both are viewed as being in the top ten of America's best presidents, held a college degree. ____True or False____
3. Since James Monroe was the only president among the first six presidents not to have earned a college degree, he supported the idea of a military academy but gave no similar support of higher education or an institution of higher education. ____True or ____False
4. The concept of public financial support for the general education of the citizenry received little to no support by the early presidents of the United States. ____True or____ False
5. Interestingly enough, only one delegate member to the Continental Congress, James Monroe, ultimately became president of the United States. ____True or ____False

ANSWER KEY

Multiple Choice

Answers to question #1 is a; #2 is c; #3 is b; #4 is d; #5 is c; #6 is a; #7 is a; #8 is e; #9 is c; #10 is d.

True or False

Answers to statement #1 is False; #2 is True; #3 is False; #4 is False; #5 is False.

Your Overall Score

15–13 correct—A president's score *****
12–10 correct—A vice-president's score****
9–7 correct—A secretary of state's score***
6–4 correct—A senator's score**
3–1 correct—A representative's score*
0 correct—Sorry, out of stars

DISCUSSION QUESTIONS

1. Thomas Jefferson's statements and legislative bills reveal his view of civic literacy. A knowledgeable citizenry was essential for assuring the rights and liberties deserved by each citizen. Review the chapter's discussion of enlightenment. What were the implications of enlightenment for educational provisions and practices?

2. Every early U.S. president emphasized the importance of an educated citizenry for sustaining a democratic republic and protecting the civil liberties of each human being. Just how does education contribute to these two democratic essentials? Be specific in your response. For example, how does education contribute to an individual's ability to participate in the process of a democratic republic?
3. Assume that you are a teacher of social studies in a middle school in the state of Nebraska. One student asks about the Monroe Doctrine and what it had to do, if anything, with the development of the state. What is your response?
4. Although education was on the minds of each of the early presidents discussed in this chapter, what factors tended to inhibit the development of public schools in the early history of the United States?
5. Although education was not mentioned in the U.S. Constitution, several amendments to the Constitution have been made over the years. No amendment, however, has centered on education, although several have had implications for teacher and student rights. Why, in your opinion, do you think that the federal government has not introduced and adopted an educational amendment that established the government's role and/or jurisdiction?

SELECTED HISTORICAL EVENT OF THIS ERA

The "Star-Spangled Banner"

The story of the "Star-Spangled Banner" serves as an interesting story to close this chapter. Most people know that it was Francis Scott Key who wrote the lyrics for America's national anthem, but may not know the rest of the story. Few persons would know that Francis Scott Key was known by his family and friends as Frank. Frank was a thirty-five-year-old lawyer who volunteered to go to Baltimore on horseback on a prisoner-exchange mission. He was carrying orders given to him by President Madison.

History reports the fact that Key was being held on a British ship until after the British attacked Baltimore. Key viewed the battle from the ship and behind the fifty-ship British fleet. A smaller flag was flown at Fort McHenry since the fort's large garrison flag was too big and heavy to hoist when being waterlogged as it were. According to a report by Leepson (2014), the larger garrison flag was hoisted after the battle and this is what Key saw the next morning. Key spent the night writing the song that some 100 years later would become the national anthem of the United States. Key wrote the verses for the song on the back of a letter that he took from his pocket; the lyrics were not given a title at the time.

Reportedly, Key's lyrics were in the Baltimore newspapers with the title, "Defence of Fort M'Henry." A Baltimore newspaper printed the song with sheet music for the first time with the title "The Star-Spangled Banner." But what about the melody? It was noted that the lyrics should be sung by the melody of "To Anacreon in Heaven." Key's poem rhyme and meter were a close match to the London song, "To Anacreon in Heaven" (Leepson, 2014). He notes that this London song served as the theme song of the upper-crust Anacreontic Society of London and a popular pub drinking song. The song contains the lyrics, "And pale beam'd the Crescent, it's splendor obscur'd / By the light of the star-spangled flag of our nation." Interestingly enough, "The Star-Spangled Banner" was not adopted until some 100 years later when the House approved the bill and the Senate followed on March 3, 1931. On the same day, President Hoover signed the document that made "The Star-Spangled Banner" the national anthem of the United States.

Clay Thompson, a writer for *Arizona Republic*, set forth an addendum to the foregoing history of the National Anthem's lyrics (2017). He noted that the lyrics of the third stanza serve as a problem. The stanza lyrics say that "and where is that band who so vauntingly swore/That the havoc of war and battle's confusion/A home and a country, should leave us no more/Their blood has washed out their foul footstep's pollution. No refuge could save the hireling and slave/from the terror of flight, or the gloom of the grave." Nevertheless, Thompson points out that historians differ in their meaning of the foregoing lyrics.

According to Thompson, some historians contend that the lyrics refer to black slaves who fled servitude and fought for the British. Other historians say it referred to German troops the British rented to build up their army. Thompson leaves it to the reader to decide.

REFERENCES

Cook, S. A., & Klay, W. E. (2014, April 20). George Washington and Enlightenment ideas on educating future citizens and public servants. *Journal of Public Affairs Education*, v. 12, n. 1, pp. 45–56.

Foley, J. P. (1900). Thomas Jefferson on politics & government: Educating the people. From a letter by Jefferson to William C. Jarvis, 1820. ME 15:278.

Gutek, G. L. (1986). *Education in the United States: An historical perspective.*, Englewood Cliffs, NJ: Prentice Hall.

Klein, C. (2014, September 12). 9 things you may not know about "The Star-Spangled Banner." *History Stories*. From the web: http://www.history.com/news/9-things-you-may-not-know-about-the-star-spangled-banner.

League of Women Voters. (2011). The history of federal government in public education. Where have we been and how did we get here? Washington, DC: Author.

Leepson, M. (2014, June 24). Star-Spangled history: 5 facts about the making of the national anthem. *Biography*.

Segarra, E. (2013, April 14). 18th century advice: Thomas Jefferson on education reform. *The Daily Signal*.

Stagg, J. C. A. (2017). Life before the presidency. From the web: https://millercenter.org/president/madison/life-before-the-presidency.

Thompson, C. (2017, September 29). Key story adds intrigue to national anthem's lyrics. *The Arizona Republic*. Section 2A. Phoenix, Arizona.

Wikipedia (2017, May 19). List of presidents of the United States of America by education. From the web: https://en.wikipedia.org/wiki/List_of_Presidents_of_the_United_States_by_education.

Zechmeister, G. (2011, July 5). Timeline of the founding the University of Virginia. An article of the *Thomas Jefferson Encyclopedia.*, Charlottesville, VA: Thomas Jefferson Foundation. From the web: https://www.monticello.org/site/research-and-collections/timeline-founding-university-virginia.

Author's Note: In writing the chapters for this book, the entire compilation of messages and papers of the presidents from 1789 to 1829 were examined. The several volumes were published by authority of the U.S. Congress as directed by James D. Richardson, a representative of the State of Virginia. The several volumes were printed by the Washington Government Printing Office in 1896.

Chapter 2

Education Views and Contributions of U.S. Presidents 1829–1877

The Era of War, Turmoil, and the New Nation

Primary chapter goal: To present the views and contributions of U.S. presidents who served in office from 1829 to 1877.

Selected historical happenings that influenced this era: First industrial revolution; Missouri Compromise; Monroe Doctrine; Emerson; Longfellow; the Alamo; California Gold Rush; *Dred Scott* decision; Lincoln-Douglas debates; Reconstruction; slavery; Civil War; Thirteenth Amendment; and Little Big Horn.

INTRODUCTION

As stated in the preface, the primary purpose of the book is to emphasize the specific views and contributions of presidents of United States relative to public school education in the United States. Research activities and readings soon led to the realization that many of the nation's presidents did not have a notable record in this regard; their speeches, writings, and legislative activities, while serving in the presidency, included little or no specific evidence of their expressed views of public education nor did their policy or legislative activities include evidence of public school dispositions.

ANDREW JACKSON
The American Revolution and New Nation Era

Andrew Jackson is ranked among the top U.S. presidents by many persons who have studied the presidency. In studying the compilations of Jackson's writings and addresses (e.g., inaugural address, executive orders, annual messages,

Andrew Jackson (1829–1857)

special messages, proclamations, veto messages, farewell addresses, and other information regarding his administration), education topics are limited. Certain statements by Jackson do infer his views on educational matters, but the words "public education" and "educated citizenry" are limited in his speeches and correspondence.

In relation to Jackson's inaugural addresses, some persons suggested that he underscored the supremacy of states' rights over federal powers. Yet others contend that Jackson was a spirited defender of federal authority. In his Farewell Address of 1837, Jackson stated, "But each state has the unquestionable right to regulate its own internal concerns according to its own pleasure, and while it does not interfere with the rights of other states or the rights of the Union, every state must be the sole judge of the measures proper to secure the safety of the citizens and promote their happiness."

The foregoing statement is set forth primarily to suggest that Jackson's lack of involvement in public education was due to his belief of state rights and the fact that education was a right delegated to the states and the people. If the federal government had intervened into the matters of a state's educational provisions, it would constitute the assumption of powers which had not been granted. In addition, Jackson was handcuffed by his adversity to the "crooked" banks that were consuming a great deal of his time.

MARTIN VAN BUREN

Although Martin Van Buren had an active and full political life, he served only one term in the presidency from 1837 to 1841. Twenty-one years before the entry date of his presidency, he served for twenty-one years as a member of the University of the State of New York Board of Regents, his only significant participation in education. One major factor for his troublesome

Martin Van Buren (1837–1841)

tenure as president was that of a great depression that occurred and left the people without work and no money to help support the economy. The record of his lifetime professional career pursuits does not include important specific views or contributions to public education other than the aforementioned service as a regent for just over two decades before his appointment as president.

WILLIAM HENRY HARRISON

William Henry Harrison was inaugurated as president of the United States on March 4, 1841, and died one month later on April 4, 1841. John Tyler was named as Harrison's vice-president. However, a review of Harrison's inaugural address and the early political activities of his life reveals no special views and/or contributions to public education. A major catastrophe and a national depression inhibited Harrison's ability to accomplish positive works.

William Henry Harrison (1841)

People were out of work and unable to purchase land or material in support of the nation's economy. In fact, Harrison has been held in low esteem as the country's president by historians although others have viewed him in a more positive manner than he is generally remembered.

JOHN TYLER

John Tyler (1841–1845)

There is little of significance that can be reported relative to John Tyler's contributions to public education. The literature and public documentation of his papers, while in office of president, give no significant evidence of his views on public education or specific actions taken relative to education and its importance to the nation in general. He did believe that the federal government should tend to its own business, not that of the states. Some would argue, perhaps, that Tyler's signing the bill that admitted Texas as a state in the union added in various ways to the expansion of education. For example, the addition of new states and territories to the United States served to foster a continuous need for new schools and a more educated citizenry.

JAMES K. POLK

James K. Polk (1845–1849)

James K. Polk served one term in the presidency from 1845 to 1849. Polk gave serious attention to the question of state and federal sovereignty. He respected the right for each state to act on its rights under the U.S. Constitution that, in turn, the states needed to be equally concerned about the limits of these rights. Specifically, in his Inaugural Address in 1845, he stated

> Each state is a complete sovereignty within the sphere of its reserved powers. The Government of the Union, acting within it delegated power is also a complete sovereignty. While the General Government should abstain from the exercise of authority, not clearly delegated to it, the States should be equally careful that in the maintenance of their rights, they do not overstep the limits of powers reserved for them.

Polk's statement would seem to make it clear that he believed that the federal government should stay clear of intervening in educational matters at state level. As noted in several previous chapter statements, education was reserved to the states. The federal government was to abstain from exercising any authority in this regard. However, implications for the future of public education in America were evident in several acts that took place in Polk's administration. One such action was the annexation of Texas into the United

States. In addition, the war against Mexico was ended and the United States gained major new properties that included almost one-half of what was then Mexico and included all which is now the Southwest of the United States, plus parts of Utah, Nevada, Wyoming, and a large portion of California.

The U.S.-Mexico Treaty guaranteed citizenship rights to everyone living in these acquired areas. In addition, the treaty gave permission for schools in these areas to use the Spanish language in their educational program. It is interesting to note that in 1998, after 150 years, this permission was rejected in California in their passing of Proposition 227 making it illegal for teachers to speak Spanish in public schools (Applied Research Center, 2013).

ZACHARY TAYLOR

Zachary Taylor (1849–1850)

Zachary Taylor died one year and four months into his office. Virtually nothing has been published relative to his views on public education nor are any public education activities prominently noted in the literature. Taylor's brief inaugural address on March 5, 1849, made no mention of education. His remarks did give attention to those matters that he viewed important as president including the command of the army and navy, treaties, the appointment of ambassadors and state officers, State of the Union reports, recommendation of measures, and to see that the necessary laws are fair and fully executed.

Taylor did not go to high school, thus had no college credits either. It is interesting to note that Taylor does not have a presidential library or shrine of any kind. In addition, he has no museum, home, or other structures commemorating his service. He did have a U.S. $1 coin with his figure minted in 2009. The coin is made of brass, not gold, and was listed for $18.99 in one advertisement on the web.

MILLARD FILLMORE

Millard Fillmore (1850–1853)

History has little to say about Fillmore in general and little to say about his views or contributions to public education in America. Fillmore was home schooled by his parents until apprenticed to a cloth maker as a young boy. At age twenty-three, he enrolled at the New Hope Academy and ultimately married his teacher who was only two years older than him. Between the years 1819 and 1823, he was involved in education as a teacher and studied law. He did earn a college degree and in 1823 was admitted to the bar.

After serving as president of the United States from 1850 to 1853, he continued to be active by participating in community projects such as the building of the first high school in Buffalo, New York, and a hospital in the same city. He toured Europe in 1855 and was offered an honorary doctorate degree in civil law by Oxford University. Fillmore turned down the offer since he felt that his educational attainments did not warrant this high honor. Nevertheless, a statute of Fillmore was erected in Buffalo, New York, next to the city hall. In addition, Fillmore, Utah, was named after him by Brigham Young for his gratitude for being named the first governor for the territory of Utah. Fillmore also served as chancellor of the University of Buffalo, which is somewhat surprising in view of the fact that Fillmore did not have a college degree. Fillmore's home in East Aurora, New York, is maintained by the Aurora Historical Society.

FRANKLIN PIERCE

It is safe to say that Franklin Pierce supported the importance of state rights. In his inaugural address in 1853, he stated that

> if the Federal Government will confine itself to the exercise of powers clearly granted by the Constitution it can hardly happen that its actions upon any question should endanger the institutions of the states or interfere with their rights to manage matters strictly domestic to the will of the people.

Franklin Pierce (1853–1857)

He also stated that "the dangers of a concentration of all powers in the general governance of a confederacy so vast as ours are too obvious to disregard." This view is most likely the reason that Pierce's attention to public school matters was not present in his deliberations. At the age of twenty, Pierce graduated from Bowdoin College in Brunswick, Maine. Reportedly, he enjoyed military life and even commanded a company of his students, one of whom was his friend Nathaniel Hawthorne, the well-known poet who was a private at the time. Interestingly enough, later as a member of the New Hampshire, he spoke against a bill that was in support of the West Point Military Academy. Two of Franklin Pierce's most telling quotes were as follows:

After the White House what is there to do but drink?

There's nothing left but to get drunk!

He obviously followed his own advice for on October 8, 1869, he died of cirrhosis of the liver at the age of 65.

JAMES BUCHANAN

James Buchanan served as president just prior to the Civil War. In his inaugural address of March 4, 1857, he underscored three major purposes to be given his attention. He hoped to extinguish the public debt, recommended a reasonable spending increase for the U.S. Navy, and wanted to create a kind spirit to all nations. No mention was made of education in the address.

James Buchanan (1857–1861)

One of Buchanan's notable quotations centered on the importance of science for making things better and improving things: "The only purpose of science is its ultimate assistance in the development of normative propositions. We seek to learn how the world works in order to make it 'better', to 'improve' things: this is as true with science as it is with social science."

ABRAHAM LINCOLN

History reports that Abraham Lincoln had less than twelve months of education in his youth; he was actually self-educated. Most every effort to list the best presidents ever in the United States lists Abraham Lincoln at the top or high on the list. Yet, his legacy tends to support the old saying that "if at first you don't succeed, try, try again." Over the several years that Abe Lincoln entered various political contests, he lost five separate elections before finally winning his first election. Among his many successes, he also encountered

Abraham Lincoln (1861–1865)

many personal and political defeats. *Abrahan Lincoln Online* shows that Lincoln:

- lost his job and was defeated for state legislature in 1832;
- failed in business in 1833;
- had a nervous breakdown in 1836;
- was defeated for Speaker in 1838;
- was defeated for nomination for Congress in 1843;
- lost renomination in 1848;
- was rejected for land officer in 1849;
- was defeated for U.S. Senate in 1854;
- was defeated for nomination for vice-president in 1856;

- again, was defeated for U.S. Senate in 1858; and
- was elected President in 1860.

One of the most far-reaching and oft-quoted educational statements of any president is Abraham Lincoln's quotations that "the leading object of government is to clear the paths of laudable pursuit for all; to afford an unfettered start and fair chance in the race of life." Although Lincoln was mainly concerned with the event of the Civil War and the matter of slavery, his views on education were meaningfully expressed in many statements and by his specific actions. See the specific quotations that follow:

> Upon the subject of education, not presumably to dictate any plan or system respecting it, I can only say that I view it as the most important subject which we as a people can be engaged in. That every man may receive at least, a moderate education, and thereby be enabled to read the histories of his own and other countries, by which he may duly appreciate the value of our free institutions countries, which may appreciate the value of our fee institutions, appears to be an object of vital importance, even on this account alone, to say nothing of the advantages and satisfaction to be derived from all being able to read the scriptures and other works, both of a religious and moral nature for themselves. For my part, I desire to see the time when education and by its means, morality, sobriety, enterprise and industry, shall become much more general than at present, and should be gratified to have it my power to contribute something to the advancement of any measure which might have a tendency to accelerate the happy period.

> It follows from this that henceforth educated people must labor. Otherwise, education itself would become a positive and intolerable evil. No country can sustain, in idleness, more than a small percentage of its numbers. The great majority must labor at something productive.

> A capacity, and taste, for reading, gives access to whatever has already been discovered by others. It is the key, or one of the keys, to the already solved problems. And not only so. It gives a relish, and facility, for successfully pursuing [yet] unsolved ones.

> Let's turn the government back into the channel in which the framers of the Constitution originally placed it.

> Always bear in mind that your own resolution to succeed is more important than any others.

> Whatever you are, be a good one. The philosophy of the school room will be the philosophy of government in the next.

> My best friend is to give me a book I have not read.

> I leave you hoping that the lamp of liberty will burn in your bosoms until there no longer shall be a doubt that all men are created equal.

Each of the foregoing quotations serves to reveal Lincoln's views on education in relation to its importance in fostering the concept of freedom, the advantages that education gives to the individual, one's personal attitude and understanding that successful outcome in one's life depends most directly on you as a person, the influence of schooling in directing the ideas one holds in life, and the belief that education should rest with the individual states as delegated by the U.S. Constitution.

Legislation of Lincoln's Time

One of the most significant educational acts of the time was the Morrill Act that was also known as the Land Grant College Act. Although the Morrill Act focused on higher education, its impact on public school programming was significant. Not only was the act a major boost for higher education in America, but it also influenced public school programs in the areas of industrial arts, agriculture, vocational education, and other industry-related courses in K–12 education. Sixty-nine colleges were funded by land grants related to the Morrill Act, including Cornell University, the Massachusetts Institute of Technology, and the University of Wisconsin at Madison.

The first Morrill Act granted 30,000 acres of public land to each state for each senator and representative in had in Congress. As a result, land grant colleges were established throughout the country. The act was first proposed in 1857 and passed Congress in 1859. We note, however, that Buchanan vetoed the act that was later signed into law by the next U.S. president, Abraham Lincoln. Other Morrill acts followed that supported the pathway for the industrial classes to gain access to higher education. As previously stated, classes in industrial arts were installed in secondary schools throughout the nation as a result of the influence of the land grant acts and the nation's need for industrial leadership.

The purpose of the Morrill Act was to establish at least one college in every state. The college, that was to be accessible to all, was to be set on a strong and perpetual foundation for improved learning. The Morrill Act opened the door for establishing colleges nationally. Although the bill focused on agriculture, engineering, and national security measures, it opened the door to the middle class of the citizenry that included both men and women. Additionally, its influence on the curriculum at the public school level is noteworthy.

The Homestead Act of 1862 established the U.S. Department of Agriculture. The Homestead Act of 1862 created the foundation for public secondary education. It provided settlers with 160 acres of survey land after the payment of filing fees and five years of continuous residence. The act helped farmers maximize the productivity of their land and farms. Eventually, 1.6 million homesteads were granted. Schools were slow to develop at the time; people lived so far apart. But the foundation was set for establishing one-room schools and encouraging some students to seek additional college work for the benefits of agriculture and mechanical arts.

ANDREW JOHNSON

Andrew Johnson (1865–1869)

Records show that Andrew Johnson was drunk while he made his vice-president's inauguration speech to Congress in 1864. The records also indicate that he fought all proposed legislation and actions that focused on eliminating slavery or improving its conditions. He was the first president to be impeached. His removal from office was based on the Tenure of Office Act that restricted the president's power to remove certain office holders without the approval of the Senate. Johnson had vetoed the bill.

An historical initiative performed by President Johnson was that of his signing of the first Department of Education legislation. Although the bill's influence on the governance of education was insignificant, the bill did fulfill the purpose of collecting data relative to public school operations. Due to considerable concern being expressed relative to this federal department's control of education within the states, a bill was passed changing the department's title to the Office of Education just one year later. Nevertheless, the federal government's Office/Department of Education has had its ups and downs from that time to the present. A brief history of the department is presented later in this chapter.

As a child, Johnson never attended a school but did participate in school debates at one school several miles from his home. He made no significant contributions to the improvement of the growing nation or to education that was expanding throughout the states.

ULYSSES S. GRANT

Ulysses S. Grant (1869–1877)

Ulysses S. Grant, actually, Hiram Ulysses Grant, historically is remembered for his generalship during the Civil War and his troubles with smoking and drinking. Later in life, Grant was diagnosed with throat cancer; his habit of heavy drinking in his early years stayed with him throughout his life. At one time, following the Mexican War, his commanding general informed him that he would have to stop drinking or resign from the service. Grant chose the second alternative.

It must be said that Grant did give some thought to education and its importance to the country. In a message to the Senate and House of Representatives on March 30, 1870, he stated that "I would therefore call upon Congress to take all means within their congressional powers to promote and encourage popular education throughout the country, and upon the people everywhere to see to it that all who possess and exercise political rights shall have the opportunity to acquire the knowledge which will make their share in the Government a blessing and not a danger. By such means the benefits contemplated by this Amendment to the Constitution be secured."

Grant was referring to the recently approved Fifteenth Amendment that prohibited the federal and state governments from denying a citizen top vote based on the citizen's race, color, or previous condition of servitude. The amendment was ratified in 1870 as one of the Reconstruction Amendments. Grant's foregoing educational statement parallels that of former presidents, including George Washington, John Adams, Thomas Jefferson, and others. It presents an especially strong statement of belief that an educated citizenry was of paramount importance protecting the liberty rights of all citizens.

Additional views of President Grant, relative to education, are found in two of his quotations as follows:

> The free school is the promoter of that intelligence which is to preserve us as a nation. If we are to have another contest in the near future of our national existence, I predict that the dividing line will not be Mason's and Dixon's, but between patriotism and intelligence on one side, and superstition, ambition, and ignorance on the other. Now in this centennial year of our national existence, I believe it a good time to begin the work of strengthening the foundation of the house commenced by our patriotic forefathers one hundred years ago, at Concord and Lexington.
>
> Encourage free schools, and resolve that not one dollar of money shall be appropriated to the support of any secretarial school. Resolve that neither the state nor nation, or both combined, shall support institutions of learning other than those sufficient to afford every child growing up I the land the opportunity of a good common school education, unmixed with sectarian, Pagan, or Atheistical tenets. Leave the matter of religion to the family altar, the church, and the private school, supported entirely by private contributions. Keep the church and the State forever separate. With these safeguards, I believe the battles which created the Army of the Tennessee will not have been fought in vain.

The provision of free schools and the rights of the citizenry to be educated were important views held by Grant. Education served to protect the rights set forth in the Constitution, including the right to vote. In any and all cases, however, schools in Grant's opinion must be nonsectarian. Not one cent of federal money was to be spent for sectarian schools. Grant is never mentioned in the literature for being an educational president. Although his statements, addresses, and letters commonly lauded the importance of schooling, his presidential activities did not reveal a concentrated educational program for America's public schools.

Nevertheless, Ulysses S. Grant is viewed by many historians as one of America's greatest military generals and one who opened the door for black persons to become U. S. citizens and participate in the ever-growing educational programs in schools throughout the nation.

POST-CHAPTER QUIZ

Multiple Choice

Directions: Circle the correct answer for each of the following ten chapter questions.

1. The First Continental Congress Land Ordinance of 1785:

    a   Centered on prohibiting any slave ownership in any of the township properties.
    b   Divided each township into three specific sections: one section in which no slavery could be practiced, one section where slavery could be practiced, and one section where slavery could be practiced if approved by the vote of white people in the township.
    c   Required that the sixteenth section of each township be reserved for the maintenance of a public school.
    d   Specified that no Negro persons could vote in any election that considered governance policy or office holding within the township.
    e   All of the above.

2. Which president of the United States of America, upon leaving the office of president, stated that "After the White House what is there to do but drink? and nothing to do but get drunk"?

    a   Ulysses S. Grant
    b   James Buchanan
    c   Millard Fillmore
    d   James K. Polk
    e   Franklin Pierce

3. Which president lost five separate elections in various political contests before being elected as president?

    a   Andrew Jackson
    b   Martin Van Buren
    c   Zachary Taylor
    d   Abraham Lincoln
    e   James K. Polk

4. One of the most significant early acts that held positive future educational development was:

    a   The Morrill Act signed by Andrew Jackson in 1829.

Education Views and Contributions: 1829–1877 47

    b Grant's presidential resolution on General Education and Citizen Rights Policy of 1869.
    c Polk's Education for the Future of America Act of 1846.
    d Fillmore's Presidential Proclamation for Free Education in 1852.
    e Lincoln's announcement of Freedom and Liberty Act of 1862.

5. Although Ulysses Grant was a highly respected military general, he:

    a Never mentioned any matters of education in his addresses, quotations, or presidential actions.
    b Believed that education, like any matter facing the nation's present or future, necessarily had to be controlled by the federal government.
    c Indicated that matters of education were best vested in the hands of parents and citizens within the various states.
    d Suggested that it was a matter of primary importance that education, as a national concern, be placed in the hands of the federal government.
    e Stated in his first address to Congress that he and the Congress had many more questions to answer and problems to be resolved than what the many states should be doing about educating their children.

6. The dates of the reconstruction period after the Civil War were from:

    a 1865 to 1877.
    b 1837 to 1841.
    c 1869 to 1867.
    d 1877 to 1881.
    e 1861 to 1865.

7. Which act was most credited for creating the foundation for public secondary education in the United States?

    a Homestead Act of 1862
    b Morrill Act of 1829
    c Land Grant Act of 1775
    d The Westward Territory Free Land Proviso in 1901
    e President Lincoln's presidential proclamation for territorial settlements in 1864

8. Which president, discussed in this chapter, most likely should be most credited for his positive views on public education and his support of policy governance for promoting public education during his life time?

    a Abraham Lincoln
    b Andrew Jackson

c Franklin Pierce
   d Millard Fillmore
   e James Buchanan

9. Which president discussed in chapter 2 lost five separate elections in various political contests before being elected to the presidency?

   a Abraham Lincoln
   b Andrew Jackson
   c Franklin Pierce
   d Millard Fillmore
   e James Buchanan

10. Which factor(s) served to inhibit the development of education within the United States between the years 1829 and 1877? Circle each entry that served either as an inhibitor or deterrent to public education during this period of the nation's history.

   a The many problems and differences that existed during the Reconstruction Era
   b The event of the Civil War
   c The many other issues and problems facing both federal and state governance leaders that required attention and resolution
   d The lack of educational programs and competent educational personnel to take the necessary leadership needed at the local and state levels
   e The continued differences among the states and its citizenry regarding the problems of determining who should be permitted as students in public schools, who should pay for the education, and the questions of what should be taught in public schools
   f None of the above
   g All of the above

True or False

1. The very first Department of Education was created in 1867 in legislation signed by Andrew Jackson. ___True or ___False
2. Although the importance of public school education was stated by several U.S. presidents between the years 1829 and 1877, no president was in favor of state or parental control of education within the states. ___True or ___False
3. The U.S.-Mexico Treaty guaranteed citizenship to everyone living in the required areas. ___True or ___False
4. In James Buchanan's Inaugural Address, he spent over one-half of his time emphasizing the importance of public education for all citizens regardless of orientation. ___True or ___False

5. The Morrill Act of 1859 focused primarily on higher education. ____ True or ____ False
6. Although the Homestead Act of 1862 focused on agriculture, it created the foundation for public secondary education in America. ____ True or ____ False
7. Although President Grant supported free school for all citizens, he was strongly opposed to any support for secretarial schools. ____ True or ____ False
8. Although Zachary Taylor died after spending only one year and four months as president, he set a record by passing some twenty presidential proclamations in supporting public education during his tenure. ____ True or ____ False
9. It is safe to say that Franklin Pierce favored the importance of state rights on public education. ____ True or ____ False
10. James Buchanan's Inaugural Address emphasized the importance of public education, the need for free public schools, and the opportunity for prospective teachers to attend free normal school education if heading for a position in teaching. ____ True or ____ False

ANSWER KEY

Multiple Choice

The answer to question #1 is c; #2 is c; #3 is d; #4 is a; #5 is c; #6 is a; #7 is a; #8 is b; #9 is a; #10 is g.

True or False

The answer to question 1 is True; #2 is False; #3 True; #4 is False; #5 is True; #6 is True; #7 is True; #8 is False; #9 is True; #10 is False.

DISCUSSION QUESTIONS

1. Examine the significance of schooling in a township as organized in the early colonial years with the concept of school wards in later years. What might you identify as similarities and primary differences?
2. This chapter mentions education and schooling. Distinguish between these two concepts.
3. Why, in your opinion, has there been so much controversy in regard to public schools being separated from any sectarian education?
4. The chapter gives rather high marks to Andrew Jackson for his views and actions relative to public education. However, Jackson's personal education consisted of only six years of basic schooling. Like many other early

presidents, he received no degrees. How might one provide some rationale for Jackson's positive views and actions relative to public education?
5. It is quite true that black slaves commonly were uneducated in terms of being able to read or write. Upon being freed, problems relating to the education of former slaves dominated the issues surrounding education in the states. What, in your opinion, were the major factors that were "pushing" for the education of black citizens: the young black people, their parents, those in federal government positions, or other conditions?
6. After studying the information provided in this chapter, what would be your pick(s) for a president(s) that could be viewed as educational presidents? Justify your response.

SELECTED HISTORICAL EVENT OF THIS ERA

The Battle of the Alamo

"Remember the Maine," "Remember Pearl Harbor," and "Remember the Alamo," are phrases echoed by the crowds to raise the spirits of Americans at times of battle against an enemy. The Battle of the Alamo took place in a Mission, which was located near the city, which now is San Antonio, Texas. About 100 troops were stationed at the Mission site when a troop of about 1,500 soldiers of Mexican army engaged the Texans into a battle that lasted for the next ten days. The Texans were far outnumbered; requested reinforcements had failed to appear. Other Texans and adventurers, including the renowned Davey Crockett, had joined the Alamo defenders. The numbers of persons in the Alamo did increase, since the Texan battle deaths were estimated to be 182 to 257 (Wikipedia, 2017).

Reportedly, Colonel James C. Neill, whose name is seldom noted in relation to the Alamo story, was the acting commander of the Alamo. He left the Alamo to recruit additional reinforcements and gather needed supplies. He left and transferred the command to cavalry officer, William B. Travis. Travis had difficulties being accepted as commander, and instead the defenders wanted James Bowie, a reputed fighter, to serve as commander. After much dissention, Travis and Bowie got together to lead the Alamo troops.

Santa Anna, the leader of the Mexican army, continued to gather additional soldiers.

The Mexican army continued to prepare for an attack. Travis knew that an attack was imminent and was said to have drawn a line in the ground and asked members of the Texan group to step beside him if they were willing to die for the Texan cause. This version of the story has been held in question, although most persons agree that Travis did give members a chance to escape before the ensuing battle took place.

The Mexicans retreated after their first attack on the Mission and once again a second attack was repulsed by the Texans. Then a third attack took place and their numbers and fire power overwhelmed the Texas fighting force. Considerable interior fighting took place and the slaughtering of the Texas force was imminent. Those Texan fighters hiding in the various barracks rooms were exposed by canon fire that blew open doors and left those inside the rooms open to gun fire and hand-to-hand combat.

Reportedly, only five to seven Texans surrendered, but these persons were ordered killed by Santa Anna anyway. Stories relative to the deaths of Crockett, Travis, and Bowie differ. Some reports tell of Crockett's surrender, while others report his death among many Mexican corpses. The end came to the Mexican siege when, on April 21, 1836, the Texan army, led by Sam Houston, attacked Santa Anna's camp in the Battle of San Jacinto. The battle was reported as being over in eighteen minutes. Many of Texan soldiers were known to call out, "Remember the Alamo."

Santa Anna's life was spared and he was forced to order his troops out of Texas, which ended the Mexican control of the province (Wikipedia, 2017).

REFERENCES

Abraham Lincoln on Line. (2017). *Lincoln's "Failures"?* From the Chronology in *Abraham Lincoln: Selected Speeches and Writings* by D. E. Fehrenbacher, ed. in 1992.

Applied Research Center. (2013, November 6). Historical timeline of public education in the US. *Race Forward.* From the web: https://www.raceforward.org/research/reports/historical-timeline-public-education-us.

Jackson, A. (1837, March 4). Farewell address. Online by G. Peters and J. T. Woolley. *The American Presidency Project.* From the web: http://www.presidency.ucsb.edu/ws/?pid=67087.

Wikipedia (2017, July 11). Battle of the Alamo. From the web: https://en.wikipedia.org/wiki/Battle_of_the_Alamo.

Author's note: The official papers of the presidents included in this chapter were used as the sources of information for the chapter's contents. For example, the specific inaugural address(es), proclamations, letters, directions for congress, and related official papers contained important information and activities of educational views and actions of the several presidents of the time. These governmental papers are viewed as *public domain documents* and available to the citizenry for informational purposes educationally.

Chapter 3

Education Legacies of U.S. Presidents 1877–1929

The Era of National Expansion, Reconstruction, and the Second Industrial Revolution

Primary chapter goal: To present the educational presidents of the United States in relation to their personal views on education and their contributions to the establishment of public education nationally.

Selected historical happenings that influenced this era: Thomas Edison's inventions; Mark Twain; Henry Ford; National Expansion and Reconstruction Era; Nikola Tesla's inventions; Prohibition; The model T; Wounded Knee; Spanish American War; Harry Houdini; Will Rogers; Panama Canal; World War I; League of Nations; Jack Johnson boxer; Charles Lindberg; stock market crash; Babe Ruth; Amelia Earhart; and Louis Armstrong.

RUTHERFORD B. HAYES

President Hayes was a strong supporter of universal education and state rights. In his inaugural address of 1877, he stated that "universal suffrage should rest upon universal education. To this end should be made the support of free schools by the state government, and if need be supplemented by legitimate aid from national authority." Thus, it was clear that he also believed in the federal government's financial support for public schools. This contention is supported by Haye's comments in his First Annual Message to Congress on December 3, 1877.

In that message, Hayes stated, "I desire also to ask your special attention to the need for adding to the efficiency of the public schools of the district by supplementing aid from the National Treasury. This is especially just, so large a number of those attending these schools are children of employees of Government." Hayes further expressed his strong support for financial

Rutherford B. Hayes (1877–1881)

aid to the states for the education of all the people in the aforementioned annual address. Federal aid for both technical and higher education support is emphasized:

> The wisdom of legislation upon the part of Congress, in aid of the States, for the education of the whole people in the branches of study which are taught in the common schools of the country is no longer a question. The intelligent judgment of the country goes still further, regarding it as both constitutional and expedient for the general Government to extend to technical and higher education such aid as is deemed essential to the general welfare and to our prominence among the enlightened and cultured nations of the world.

In expressing his personal judgments relative to governmental support for education, he noted his concern for the success of a free government without the intelligence of persons who are in the source of power. At that time in history, 140 years ago, Hayes pointed out that approximately 15 percent of the nation's entire voting population was unable to read or write. Hayes stated publicly that he would sign any appropriate congressional measures that supplemented local systems of education in all the states. In addition, he expressed his support for the establishment of universities for the benefit of the entire country.

In his Fourth Annual Message to Congress in 1880, Hayes noted that industrial training was attracting deserved attention, and that college instruction, theoretical, and practical instruction, agriculture and mechanical arts, and recently established government schools for the instruction of Indian youth were gaining steadily in the public's estimation.

Of special interest is President Hayes' views about the education of Indians. For example, he expressed the opinion that Indians were more peaceable when their children were in school. He stated that expressions from Indians themselves indicated that there was an increasing desire belonging to comparative wild tribes to have their children educated. He was especially pleased with the activity of taking fifty Indian boys and girls to the Hampton Normal Agricultural Institute where they had training in English and agriculture. Upon completion of the training, the Indian students returned to their tribes and served as interpreters and instructors and set examples for others in the tribe.

The record indicates that Rutherford B. Hayes gave his best to promote the common schools and higher education during his tenure as president. His concerns for the education of the American Indian were revealed additionally in his addresses and letters. He held a similar view of the importance of education for the welfare of each citizen and the future of the nation. He believed that universal suffrage rested upon universal education. Universal suffrage referred to the right to vote of all citizens except minors. This end is to be achieved, he believed, when liberal and universal provisions were made for the support of free public schools.

In his Second Annual Message to Congress on December 2, 1878, President Hayes expressed his pleasure with the report of the commissioner of the Bureau of Education. He underscored his belief that the free common school was being looked upon as the resource for the advancement of the people in their requisite knowledge and appreciation of their rights and responsibilities as citizens. Once again, he mentioned the importance of the federal government to supplement national aid for local systems of education in the several states. President Hayes' support efforts for education were at top on his list of priorities while in office as president.

Nevertheless, he expressed his frustration with the growing demands regarding education and other dimensions required in his role as president. As he stated, "I am loaded down to the guards with educational, benevolent, and other miscellaneous public work. I must not attempt to do more. I cannot without neglecting imperative duties." Due to his short time in office, it is somewhat difficult to assess Hayes' actual education contributions; his beliefs, however, were specific in its support.

JAMES A. GARFIELD

James A. Garfield (1881)

James A. Garfield served as president just short of four months. He was shot by a person who reportedly denied him a position of consul in Paris. Nevertheless, some researchers contend that Garfield had the potential for contributing positively to education nationally. His college education at Williams College led to a teaching position at Western Reserve Institute in 1857. Just one year later, he was selected as president for that institution (Craig, 2017). In his inaugural address of March 1881, he emphasized the need for the education of former slaves. Garfield pointed out that the census already has "sounded the alarm" for the high tide of ignorance that has risen among the voters. Specifically, he stated that

> to the South this question is of supreme importance. But the responsibility for the existence of slavery did not rest upon the South alone. The nation itself is responsible for the extension of the suffrage, and is under special obligation to

aid in removing the illiteracy which it has added to the voting population. For the North and South alike there is but one remedy. All the constitutional power of the nation and of the States and all the volunteer forces of the people should be surrendered to meet this danger the savory influence of universal education.

Garfield proposed a universal system of education strongly supported financially by the federal government. Reportedly, he lost interest in African-American rights and his financial proposal could not find support in Congress at the time (Wikipedia, 2017).

One additional mention of how he viewed the importance of education is illustrated by his comment that next in importance to freedom and justice is popular education, without which neither freedom nor justice can be permanently maintained. Garfield's comment carries with it a similar significance of the more well-known quotation of Thomas Jefferson, when he said: "A nation that expects to be ignorant and free, expects what never has or never will be."

In his early years, Garfield showed his independence and initiative for supporting his own education and intelligently taking the unpopular side of a question and winning the cause. He took strong stands against polygamy, slavery, and the questionable practices of the civil service at the time. Garfield is credited with the reform of civil service during his brief term in the presidency. The record shows that Garfield served on the board of trustees for Hiram College and became the president of that institution in 1857. He also served on the board of trustees of Hampton University.

As previously noted, President Garfield was assassinated just less than four months after being elected to that high office. The following is one of Garfield's own quotations: "Assassination can be no more guarded against than death by lightning, and it is best not to worry about either."

CHESTER A. ARTHUR

A twenty-nine-page article on the web included a life history of Chester A. Arthur (Wikipedia, 2017). The article included only one mention of education by noting that Arthur had served at one time as a full-time teacher and later served as a principal in a school in Cohoes, New York. The record does reveal that Arthur did serve as a teacher when he was only a college sophomore.

In what was the shortest Inaugural Address of any president to date, he made no mention of education. Yet Arthur was especially efficient in other responsibilities assigned to him in various political positions and in his law practice. One source spoke of Arthur's effectiveness by stating that "his name very seldom rises to the surface of metropolitan life and yet moving like a

Chester A. Arthur (1881–1885)

mighty undercurrent this man in the last ten years has done more to mold the course of the Republican Party than any other one man in the country" (Reeves, 1972, 310). One must wonder what Arthur might have accomplished if his attention would have been focused on public school education.

Arthur's views on education are difficult to find in the literature. He was effective in promoting or criticizing a cause or proposal. His private life had its downs as well. He did have an opinion about his life outside the presidency. Specifically, he stated that "I may be the President of the United States, but my private life is nobody's damned business."

GROVER CLEVELAND

Statements concerning Grover Cleveland's lack of a college education by writers tend to be misleading relative to his accomplishments in office (Graff, 2017). For example, Graff states that the deficiency of not having a college education left Cleveland unfamiliar with the great ideas of history; thus, he never developed a national ideological direction during his presidency. Graff

Grover Cleveland (1885–1889)

also notes that not having a college education was "almost unique among the nation's presidents." In fact, however, nearly one-third (27.3 percent) of the nation's presidents have not held a college degree. Non-college-degree presidents include Washington, Lincoln, T. Roosevelt, Jackson, and Monroe, who commonly are listed among the nation's best presidents.

Cleveland's views and contributions to public school education indeed were limited. At one time in his early life, he did serve as a teacher in a school for the blind in New York. After leaving his second presidency in 1897, he retired to his home in Princeton, New Jersey, and served as a trustee of Princeton University until his death in 1908. According to the record, Cleveland's last words were, "I have tried so hard to do my best."

BENJAMIN HARRISON

Benjamin Harrison's education legacy in regard to public schools is limited. The record indicates that he worked diligently for financial aid especially for veterans and the education for the children of freed slaves. His success in this regard was limited. As Harrison stated, "When and under what conditions is the black man to have a free ballot? When is he in fact to have those full civil

Benjamin Harrison (1889–1893)

rights which have been his in law?" His proposals to secure a federal budget reached $1 billion for the first time during his term. The increases in federal funding overall led to the critics' moniker of the "Billion-Dollar Congress." Such criticism severely limited his efforts to provide for additional education funding as well.

Harrison's legacy is virtually void of interests regarding public education; he, perhaps, was too busy with the politics of the time.

THEODORE ROOSEVELT

Theodore Roosevelt is viewed by historians as being among the nation's leading presidents. His two-term presidency, however, focused on such matters as anti-trust laws, railroad powers relative to railroad rates, defense matters that centered on building up the U.S. Navy, and serving as the steward for the preservation of the nation's natural resources. T. Roosevelt's strong efforts in

Theodore Roosevelt (1901–1909)

the area of appreciation for and preservation of the nation's natural resources resounded in the curricula of the nation's public schools. Yet, today, attempts to alter the status of the nation's parks, recreational areas, protected lands, and water resources meet strong resistance on the part of the nation's citizenry.

Gutek (1986) makes special note of Roosevelt's contributions to rural renewal, enthusiasm for improving the nation's rural life in initiating the National Commission of Country Life, and appointing Liberty Hyde Bailey to chair the commission. Bailey was a professor, dean, and noted expert of agriculture at Cornell University, where he focused on scientific agriculture. The implications for education in America's education centered on schooling purposes that focused on the specific conditions of rural life, the present needs of the farm and the farm community, and the paramount importance of agricultural education.

As a result of the foregoing efforts, the Smith-Lever Act of 1914 was enacted that led to the development of extended programs of agricultural education, extension courses, and a new emphasis on home economics and agricultural programs in public school curricular programs. Teacher preparation programs gave new attention to nature study and agriculture. Programs on agriculture were extended to schools in the city as well as rural areas. Future Farmers of America (FFA) chapters were established in most every school program with the help of federal monetary support of the Smith-Lever Act.

T. Roosevelt is one of four national presidents whose image is engraved on Mount Rushmore in Colorado. He is consistently named in the listing of the ten best presidents by historians. His public record of views on agricultural education and their related contributions to public school curriculum and higher education programs serve in a positive way for the public school improved programs in home economics, nature studies, and FFA programs throughout the nation.

WILLIAM H. TAFT

William H. Taft (1909–1913)

Statements by William H. Taft would indicate that he favored the local control of public education. In his Inaugural Address of March 4, 1909, he stated,

"I believe there ought to be choice, so that parents can choose within the public school system." On another occasion, he stated that "I am not in favor of having government do anything that private citizens can do for themselves."

Although Taft held somewhat positive views regarding the education of the Negro and Indian populations, his notion of education for these citizens tended to be limited. He viewed education as a positive vehicle for Indians to become assimilated into the population. He stressed that Indian and Negro education should be elementary and largely focused on industrial knowledge.

He told Congress that the need for higher education for Indians was very limited. In his March 4, 1909, Inaugural Address, he expressed the view that in the South, there was a stronger feeling than ever among the intelligent well-to-do and influential element, in favor of industrial education of the Negro and encouragement of the race to make themselves useful members of the community by working on the farm and in the shop. Yet he told Congress that "the argument that somehow we've got to get rid of minority scholarships so that we can have a free and fair America implies that we have a colorblind society where minorities are equal in their pursuit of funds to go to school."

In any case, however, Taft was of the opinion that unless education promotes character making, unless it helps to build men to be more moral, more just to their fellows, more law abiding, and more discriminately patriotic and public spirited, it was not worth the trouble taken to furnish it.

President Taft was kept busy while focusing on the reorganization of the state department, tariff matters, foreign matters, anti-trust politics, domestic politics, and other governmental matters. After leaving the president's office in 1913, he returned to Yale University as a professor. In 1921, President Harding appointed Taft to his lifetime pursuit as chief justice of the U.S. Supreme Court. He resigned the position in 1930 and died in the same year.

WOODROW WILSON

Inaugural addresses, letters, quotations, and proclamations by Woodrow Wilson, for the most part, are centered on matters other than education, especially public schools. If not for the Smith-Hughes Act of 1917, it would be difficult to identify any other significant views or contributions that Wilson made to public education in the United States. Since Woodrow Wilson did serve as president of Princeton University from 1902 to 1910, this record and his other educational activities tie him more directly to higher education. One major exception, however, is that of Wilson's signing of the Smith-Hughes Act of 1917.

The Smith-Hughes Act enacted by Congress and signed by President Wilson in 1917 is given consideration in this section due to its significant impact on education and curricular programs in the nation's schools from 1917 to the

Woodrow Wilson (1913–1921)

present time. This act is additionally significant due to the fact that it was the first act that authorized the federal government oversight to a portion of the high school curriculum. That is, the act gave national approval of a student program of vocational education in the public schools nationally.

The Smith-Hughes Act provided federal aid to the states for the purpose of promoting precollegiate vocational education in agriculture, industrial trades, and home economics. The act was viewed as being especially important for meeting the present shortages of skilled labors needed in the growing industrial society. The act's value was vested in fostering the importance of providing an opportunity for workers to advance in industrial work and underscoring the basic value of work itself in American society. It provided a basis for dignifying economic values of labor and competing industrially with other nations. The new vocational curriculum provided new student interests and learning opportunities.

On the other hand, like most all new legislation, the Smith-Hughes Act had its detractors. For example, where should such vocational education take place? In addition, many persons argued that the act would serve only to further segregate students in school programs. How was vocational education to be interpreted for female students? Should female students be prepared to serve in the industrial areas of millinery and garment work or be better prepared to work with a family in the home? According to Steffes (2014), school vocational programs commonly lacked the student population that had been predicted and also did not produce the economic benefits anticipated for the individual student.

In addition, critics pointed out that the vocational programs provided by the public schools did not keep up with the actual needs of industrial organizations. Racial segregation was another criticism of the public school vocational program; it not only segregated students by gender but also often separated them by race and perceived ability. Nevertheless, vocational/technical programs continue in most every public school in America, although some are housed in facilities other than the local secondary school buildings.

Program activities such as the Future Farmers of America Act of 1928, the 1950 Federal Charter of the FFA, the Carl Perkins Vocational and Technical Education Act of 1984, the U.S. Department of Education/National FFA Organization Memorandum of Understanding of 2008, and the National Quality Program Standards for Secondary (Grades 9–12) Agriculture Education in 2015 are examples of the continued educational efforts within the nation to deliver high-quality agriculture programs in schools across the nation.

WARREN G. HARDING

Warren G. Harding served at Executive Office of President of the United States from March 4, 1921 to 1923. His Inaugural Address of March 4, 1923, took place approximately three years after the end of World War I. He spoke mainly of the need to recognize the order of the new world including the need to seek the ideas of world opinion, world understanding, dealing with the aftermath of war, business readjustments, tax burdens, tariffs, and other conditions needing careful attention. Yet, only one brief mention of education in America was stated: "And we want to provide that no selfish interest, no material necessity, no lack of opportunity shall prevent the gaining of that education so essential to best citizenship."

We note that Harding spent only two years and 151 days in the office of president before his death in 1923. Thus, Warren's education legacy is limited. He did comment at one time that "every student has the ability to be a successful learner." This contention is heard commonly in contemporary

Warren G. Harding (1921–1923)

educational programs today such as George H. W. Bush's "No Child Left Behind" (NCLB) legislation of 2001 discussed later in chapter 5.

Most any adult living in the 1960s will remember the statement, "Ask not what the country can do for you, ask what you can do for your country." Interestingly enough, President John Kennedy's foregoing statement had its parallel that was stated by President Harding some forty years earlier. Harding stated, "We need more citizens who are less concerned about what their government can do for them, and more concerned about what they can do for their country."

Unfortunately, the presidency of Warren Harding has been criticized historically for lack of achievements and dishonesty that took place within government operations during his tenure. He was accused of appointing committee members who were dishonest and unqualified for the tasks assigned to them. Warren's sudden death in 1923 reportedly was due to a heart attack. Other reasons, far less rational, included possible suicide, suspicion of poisoning by his wife, and malpractice by his physicians. In any case, Warren Harding's public school education legacy relative to personal views and important contributions is void. Harding has one "distinction": he is on the top or near the top of every listing of "America's Worst Presidents" who we researched.

JOHN CALVIN COOLIDGE: "SILENT CAL"

John Calvin Coolidge (1923–1929)

If one is searching for Calvin Coolidge's views and contributions regarding public school education, the search for the most part would be in vain. However, the search is likely to result in an interesting review of Coolidge's political history and his oft times humorous outcomes. For example, his reputation as a man of few words and name reference of "Silent Cal" are exemplified by the story of a woman who sat next to him at a dinner. She was reported to say to him that she had made a bet that she could get more than two words from him. Calvin reportedly replied, "You lose" (Hannaford, 2013). On another occasion, a lady who was informed that Coolidge had died, was reported to say, "How can they tell?" (Greenberg, 2006).

At one time in his life, Coolidge served as the mayor of Northampton, Massachusetts, at which time between 1910 and 1911 he increased teachers' salaries. In a previous election of 1904, Coolidge suffered a defeat in his effort for becoming a member of the Northampton school board. Both happenings do reveal some interest of Coolidge in public school education. It is interesting to note that Coolidge commonly is not among the historians' lists of worst presidents nor is he commonly listed among the best presidents. It is clear that he is not among the nation's educational presidents. Coolidge left the presidency in 1929 and died four years later in 1933 at age sixty-one.

POST-CHAPTER QUIZ

1. This chapter includes nine U.S. presidents who served between 1887 and 1929. With the possible exception of Hayes, Theodore Roosevelt, Garfield, and Wilson, public school education interests from the federal level tend to be limited. What major factors during this national expansion and reconstruction period were in evidence that tended to inhibit a president's attention to other matters such as public school education?
2. Give thought to the matter of reconstruction and its status in the South as related to education for the black citizen. What might one expect would be needed by the federal government to meet the educational needs of freed black citizens during the reconstruction period? What information in this chapter shows evidence of such leadership by the nation's presidents during this time period?
3. Woodrow Wilson held a PhD degree and served as the president of Princeton University. How would you assess Wilson's educational views and contributions to public schools in view of his personal accomplishments in scholarship and educational administration in higher education?
4. What were the key elements of Rutherford B. Hayes' educational philosophy?
5. Review the early development of vocational/industrial education as viewed by presidential leaders relative to black education during the reconstruction period. Assess the prevailing views of presidents who served during the era included in this chapter. What conclusions did you reach?
6. In view of the general status of education in America at the end of the Reconstruction Era, what kinds of leadership might one expect to see by the nation's presidents relative to public school education in the United States?

Answers Key

Question #1—Factors that inhibited attention to and implementation of positive programs of public school education. Inhibiting factors included continued prejudice regarding Indian and black citizens, workload expressed by some presidents, problems of illiteracy that existed, lack of congressional support for such programs, unfortunate assassinations that took place, lack of higher education by some presidents, increase of federal expenditures or other purposes and projects, concept of state responsibility for funding public school education, lack of positive results for funds expended for agriculture education at the local school level, major focus on business adjustments, dishonesty in governmental practices, and others.

Question #2—What would be the expectations for positive public school education support by the federal government during this era? Among the factors needing direct attention were the lack of prepared teachers for elementary and secondary education programs, widespread illiteracy among the population without sufficient teaching staff, lack of funding, administrative leadership preparation for common school effectiveness, questions regarding the purposes of universal education and which students should attend, problem of going to school, and the need of youth help to run the farm.

Question #3—Consideration of Woodrow Wilson's higher education degrees in relation to his actual views and specific contributions to public school education. There is no question that the passing of the Smith-Hughes Act relative to agriculture/vocational education during Wilson's term in office was an historical highlight in public school curriculum programs. Since the passing of this act in 1927, industrial arts, vocational education, agriculture education, and FAA activities have been evident in public school program activities. Although the legislation was drafted by Sen. Hoke Smith and Rep. D. M. Hughes, it passed Congress and received the approval signature of Woodrow Wilson.

Question #4—What were the key factors in Rutherford B. Hayes' educational philosophy? President Hayes was indeed an educational president. He demonstrated strong support for universal education and the implementation of state rights. Hayes believed in state rights but recommended strong financial support by the federal government. A strong elementary and secondary school program should serve as the foundation for higher educational programs. Intelligent individuals are essential for supporting free government. Local school programs should be established in all states that include industrial training, agricultural, and industrial arts in their curriculum. The education of Indian citizens is of importance.

Question #5—Review the development of vocational/industrial education views by presidents relative to the black population during the Reconstruction Era. In most every case, presidents who served in office during the Reconstruction Era saw the need for improved vocational/industrial education. It was common for presidents to favor such programs at both the public school level and for instructional programs in higher education. However, the literature suggests that some leaders viewed vocational education as needed by the black population since it was more relevant for their talents and skill levels. William H. Taft, for example, personally expressed this troublesome view.

Question #6—In view of the conditions facing American toward the end of the Reconstruction Era, what kinds of leadership might one expect to see by the nation's presidents relative to public school education? History writes that significant money problems with the use of greenbacks rather than gold coins became more than troublesome. Bank failures and bankruptcies were prevalent. Poor and incompetent presidential leadership resulted in corrupt business practices. In addition, segregation continued in the South and nationally, and the civil rights promised to some citizens crumbled. In brief, after-reconstruction was termed as being a staggered process.

However, black citizens' involvement in politics increased in spite of the evidence of the carpet baggers who drifted from the North to the South for the reported purposes of modernizing the South. This group included businessmen, professionals, teachers, and preachers. By 1929, banks failed and America's greatest depression began and lasted for the next several years.

DISCUSSION QUESTIONS

1. Presidents who served in office during the era discussed in this chapter tended to support public education. Why was this support so prominent at this time in history? What era factors would tend to foster such positive educational support?
2. The concept of choice within the public school system was voiced by national presidents more than 100 years ago. Discuss how this concept of choice has continued in the minds of many persons over time. What factors have served to inhibit and/or promote the concept of educational choice?
3. Review the section "The Education Legacy of Woodrow Wilson" in the chapter. How would you assess his public school contributions in view of the fact that he held a doctoral degree and served as the president of a major university in America?

SELECTED HISTORICAL EVENT OF THIS ERA

The Real "Baby Ruth"

A large percentage of the population would remember Babe Ruth, the Yankee baseball star of the 1930s, and many people have enjoyed a Baby Ruth candy bar. But, how did the name of the Baby Ruth candy bar come about? Was it named after the star baseball player? Christopher Klein (2014), Leah Zeldes (2011), and perhaps others have written about the somewhat puzzling history of this candy bar. Others have claimed that the Curtiss Candy Company's first product was a candy bar named Kandy Kake. The bar was reintroduced in 1921 with a new name, Baby Ruth, reportedly named after Ruth Cleveland, the first-born daughter of President Grover Cleveland. The candy bar became a great success in the market.

The naming of the candy bar after Ruth Cleveland becomes somewhat dubious since she had died over seventeen years before the Baby Ruth bar was first on the market. Others claim that the candy bar was named for the Yankee player, Babe Ruth, but used without his permission. Thus, the matter of royalty payments to Babe Ruth became a legal matter of concern. Yet, another version that claimed the naming of the candy bar came forward. That is, another person, Tom Burnam (1980), claimed that the candy bar was named after a granddaughter of Mr. and Mrs. George Williamson, candymakers who were said to have developed the original formula for the bar and sold it to the Curtiss Candy Company.

According to Klein (2014), knowing that the candy bar was now selling in the millions of dollars and with Babe himself looming as a baseball great, Babe Ruth decided to go into the candy business himself. A picture of Ruth was shown on a candy wrapper with the slogan of "Babe Ruth's Own Candy: Ruth's Home Run, 5 cents." A law suit followed, *George H. Ruth Candy Co. v. Curtiss Candy Co.*; but Ruth lost the case after the patent court ruled against him. Nevertheless, the Baby Ruth candy bar flourished after the legal rulings with its marketing activities and connections to professional baseball activities. Reportedly, the Baby Ruth candy bar became the official candy bar of Major League Baseball in 2006.

REFERENCES

Burnam, T. (1980). *More misinformation*. Reno, Nevada: Ty Crowell Company.

Craig, B. (2017). James Garfield: "The Education President." Miller Center, University of Virginia, Charlottesville, VA. From the web: millercenter.org/james-garfield-education-president.

Graff, H. F. (2017). Grover Cleveland: Impact and legacy. Miller Center, University of Virginia, Charlottesville, VA. From the web: https://millercenter.org/president/cleveland/impact-and-legacy.

Greenberg, D. (2006). *Calvin Coolidge*. New York: Time Books.

Gutek, G. L. (1986). *Education in the United States: An historical perspective*. Englewood Cliffs, NJ: Prentice-Hall.

Hannaford, P. (2013). *The quotable Calvin Coolidge: Sensible words for a new century*. Bennington, VT: Images from the Past, Inc.

Klein, C. (2014, September 25). Babe Ruth v. Baby Ruth. *History Stories*.

Reeves, T. C. (1972, Summer). The search for the Chester Alan Arthur papers. *The Wisconsin Magazine of History*, 55 (4): 310–319.

Steffes, T. L. (2014, June 9). Smith-Hughes Act, United States 1917. In *Encyclopedia of Education Reform and Dissent*. Edited by T. Hunt, J. Carper, T. J. Lasley II, & C. D. Raisch. From the web: DOI: http://dx.doi.org/10.4135/9781412947403.n409.

Wikipedia. (2017, July 31). James A. Garfield. From the web: https://en.wikipedia.org/wiki/James_A._Garfield.

Zeldes, L. A. (2011, July 27). Named for slugger or president's kid, candy is Chicago's baby. *Dining Chicago*. From the web: http://www.diningchicago.com/blog2011/06/27chicagos-baby-ruth/.

Chapter 4

Education Views and Contributions of U.S. Presidents 1929–1977

The Era of Depression, War, Postwar, and the New Millennium

Primary chapter goal: To identify the educational views and contributions of U.S. presidents in regard to public school education in America from 1929 to 1977.

Selected historical happening that influenced this era: The New Deal and World War II; postwar America; Albert Einstein; Adolf Hitler; Jesse Owens; Joe Louis; Pearl Harbor; *Little Orphan Annie*; "I Want You;" Joe Foss; Audie Murphy; *Gone with the Wind*; Truman and the bomb; Douglas MacArthur; Walter Cronkite; Jackie Robinson; JFK assassination; *Brown v. Board of Education*; Mickey Mantle; Woodstock; Space race; Apollo 8; the astronauts; Martin Luther King; Jr.; Nixon and Watergate; Vietnam; Nixon's resignation; Iran hostage crisis; and civil rights.

Fourteen individuals served the U.S. presidency during the years 1929 to 1977, and some faced the serious depression of the late 1920s and early 1930s, a world war, postwar reconstruction, new thrusts in public education and serious events of terrorism. At the time of this writing, America was faced with internal political dissension, verbal threats of nuclear war, terrorism, and the matter of educational choice that included the privation of public education and major differences on immigration policies. Herbert Hoover was the first president to deal with the failure of banks in America and the following problems of unemployment and poverty in America that fell upon the country in 1929.

HERBERT HOOVER

Herbert Hoover served as president of the United States during one of the world's worst economic disasters in the nation's history. The stock market

Herbert Hoover (1929–1933)

crash, bank failures, drought, purchasing problems, economic policies with other countries, and other conditions were among the serious problems facing the nation at the outset of Hoover's presidency. Hoover's inaugural address to Congress on March 4, 1929, included a significant statement of his views and hopes for public education in America. In that address, he stated:

> Although education is primarily a responsibility of the States and local communities, and rightly so, yet the Nation as a whole is vitally concerned in it development everywhere to the highest standards and to complete universality. Self-government can succeed only through an instructed electorate. Our objective is not simply to overcome illiteracy. The government has marched far beyond that. The more complex the problems of the Nation become, the greater is the new for more and more advanced instruction. Moreover, as our numbers increase and our life expands with science and invention, we must discover more and more leaders in every walk of life. We cannot hope to succeed in directing this increasing complex civilization unless we can draw all the talent of leadership from the whole people. One civilization after another has been wrecked upon the attempt to secure sufficient leadership from a single group or class. If we would prevent the growth of class distinctions and would constantly refresh our leadership with the ideals of our people, we must draw constantly from the general mass. The full opportunity for every boy and girl to rise through the selective processes of education can alone secure to us this leadership.

Hoover expressed his personal appreciation for public school education on several occasions.

At one time, he stated that "the opportunities of America opened out to me the public schools. They carried me to the professional training of American university. I began by working with my own hands for my daily bread." At another time, he noted that "my country owes me nothing. . . . It gave me schooling, independence, opportunity for service and honor." His view of the significance of the public school was shown in his statement that "no greater nor more affectionate honor can be conferred on an American than to have a public school named after him."

The record shows that Hoover's contributions to public education were impressive. Truslow (2013) discusses several important contributions of Hoover, which were designed to improve public education. For example, at one time in his administration, Hoover increased the federal budget to include children's programs. On one occasion, Hoover stated, "We need to add to the three R's, a fourth—RESPONSIBILITY." He hosted the first White House Conference on Child Health and Protection. His concerns for children and youth were extended even after he left the office of president. In 1936, three years after his term of president, he became chairman of the Boys' Clubs of America and remained in that work for twenty-five years.

Truslow (2013) notes further that Hoover worked for improved conditions for the Indian population that included better schools and educational opportunities. Educational and health benefits for employees of prisons were initiated, and a special school for the training of prison employees was established. Perhaps Hoover's most significant leadership contribution for children was his work as cofounder of the United Nations Children's Fund (UNICEF). UNICEF serves as a world advocate for all children's health, welfare, and rights.

UNICEF was created in 1946 by Herbert Hoover and Maurice Pate in response to diseases of World War II as the internal development support agency of the United Nations General Assembly. The fund helps 192 countries around the world with education including classroom rehabilitation, learning materials, and teacher preparation.

It would be an oversight not to mention Hoover's efforts to harness electric energy by promoting the building of the Hoover Dam. In addition, he worked with Canada in developing the St. Lawrence waterway and was instrumental in building the San Francisco Bay Bridge and also the Los Angeles Aqueduct system.

Due to the disastrous problems encountered by the depression from 1929 to 1933, Hoover's presidency commonly is rated as being inefficient and unsuccessful. Yet, many of his educational accomplishments exceeded those of other presidents and his education contributions are present in many contemporary practices. His positive perspectives of the importance of an educated citizenry are revealed in his inaugural address set forth at the outset of the chapter.

FRANKLIN D. ROOSEVELT (FDR)

Franklin D. Roosevelt (1933–1945)

"Democracy cannot succeed unless those who express their choice are prepared to choose wisely. The real safeguard of democracy, therefore, is education." This quotation, perhaps, best expresses Franklin Roosevelt's views of the importance of an educated citizenry. He further expressed support to the public schools in his statement that "the school is the last expenditure upon which America should be willing to economize." A doctoral dissertation completed by Permeil Dass, a graduate student of Georgia State University, centered on answering the following questions: Did his administrative decision support public schools? What was FDR's policy toward federal aid to education and why? Dass discusses in depth Roosevelt's relief programs, one of which was the Civilian Conservation Corps (CCC) that was supported with an approximate budget of $323 million.

The primary purposes of the CCC program were to reduce the unemployment of young people, make them more productive, conserve natural resources, and provide educational activities that fostered character building for all participants in the program. It is beyond the scope of this chapter to detail all of the many problems faced within the CCC program politically and educationally, but differences in the CCC program content were prominent. Was the program to focus on the reduction of illiteracy that was evident among the participants through educational program activities or to educate them on the subject of forestry and the conservation of natural resources?

Reportedly, FDR did not want the educational program to overshadow CCC's conservation plan. From a political point of view, the focus of providing participants' activities that were more physical in nature than educational training was more acceptable. Yet, the pressures for providing an educational program for CCC participants resulted in the establishment of an educational program that originally was not mandatory for all enrollees in the program. The stated purposes of the education program as reported in Dass' dissertation (2014) were as follows: (1) elimination of illiteracy, (2) removal of deficiencies in common school subjects, (3) training on the job, (4) cultural and general education, (5) health and safety education, (6) character and citizenship training, and (7) assist enrollees in finding employment.

According to Gower (1967), of the enrollees in CCC educational programs in 1934, 20 percent were learning literacy and basic skills, 30 percent were working on high school diplomas, 7 percent were taking college-level courses, 12 percent were enrolled in arts and crafts courses, and 30 percent were involved in vocational training. The cost of the educational program was estimated at $3.45 million annually. As time went by, funding for the CCC educational program became problematic. Reportedly, Roosevelt's support of the program dwindled and ultimately Congress cut the CCC program in 1942 after nine years of its operation.

According to a report by Couch (1989), by 1940, President Roosevelt's Works Administration Program (WAP) had constructed 4,383 new school buildings across the nation and made repairs and additions to more than 30,000 others. In addition, he signed into law the Servicemen's Readjustment Act of 1944, best known as the GI Bill.

When the GI Bill of 1943 comes to mind, its purpose of giving servicemen and women the opportunity of resuming their education, completing technical/vocational training, or taking appropriate refresher courses comes to mind. Although this purpose was most important to thousands of military veterans who took advantage of the bill's provisions, the bill had five other purposes as well. None of the other five purposes focused directly on education. For example, one additional purpose of the bill was to authorize the construction of all necessary additional hospital facilities. Another stated purpose was to provide unemployment allowances to veterans who were unable to find work.

Another educational contribution of Franklin Roosevelt was the National Youth Administration (NYA) program. Dass (2014) traces the history of the NYA program in his doctoral dissertation mentioned previously. Both Franklin Roosevelt and his wife, Eleanor, were greatly concerned about America's youth who were unable to afford the cost of a college education and found it difficult to find employment. Youths, facing the present insecurity of life, formed an organization, the American Youth Congress (AYC), in 1934. Mrs. Roosevelt became interested in the AYC activities, some of which were highly questionable, and ultimately the organization to work cooperatively with the White House. As a result, the AYC became the NYA, which worked closely with the New Deal philosophy of President Roosevelt.

Ultimately, the NYA program was placed in the U.S. Office of Education and directed by Secretary Studebaker. Further problems resulted with this movement and further adjustments in the administration of the program were established. Unfortunately, the program was placed under Henry Hopkins, director of the WKA. The National Education Association (NEA) strongly objected. FDR explained to the NEA that the NYA program was to provide relief to youth and that Williams under Hopkins was more experienced to do so.

After the years went by and all was said and done, the NEA resumed control of the NYA program. Both the NEA and the American School Administrators Association (AASA) called for the termination of both the CCC and the NYA programs. The CCC program was closed officially in 1942; the NYA program necessarily focused on national defense to support the war effort. It ended officially by an act of Congress in 1943.

In 1933, Federal Emergency Relief Administration (FERA) created the Emergency Educational Program (EEP). In the depression years of the 1930, thousands of teachers were unemployed and about to depend on relief support, schools in rural areas were in need of repair, social services were needed for preschool children, and vocational training was needed to provide the skills necessary for employment. The EEP programs were offered in a variety of business, industrial, and trades areas and often taught by uncertified persons who had the experience needed to help others gain the necessary skills.

Adult education courses were available to individuals who were on relief, rehabilitation services were available to persons with special needs, and nursery schools also were part of the program, as were programs for college aid. Problems and differences regarding the program activities and control of the EEP activities were ongoing. Members of Roosevelt's Advisory Committee on Education were of the opinion that educational programs such as those provided by EEP should be placed within the jurisdiction of public schools.

It is clear that the Franklin Roosevelt's terms in the presidency were filled with decisions relative to the relief of the depression's damages and the needs to improve on the struggling status of humanity.

Roosevelt's New Deal educational programs were created to help people be prepared for and find work. The lack of effective vocational programs for youth and unemployed workers, the growing numbers of youth who were absent from schooling, and effective programs for meeting these problems brought about relief programs that were centered on obviating these problems but were not directly focused on resolving the matters of illiteracy and extending the knowledge of children and youth.

Such programs as the CCC, NYA, and EEP were established by Roosevelt that held the purpose of dealing with relief by supporting work camps, vocational training, and youth development. Such programs were "instructed" by uncertified personnel, individuals who shared their experience in relation to their work knowledge. Pressures were brought about by education groups to turn the control of these programs over to them. The record shows that Roosevelt did not trust educators to do the job as he wanted it to be. Historians report that Roosevelt did not have good feelings toward educators. Educators and educational associations commonly were overlooked as the controllers of education-related programs in Roosevelt's administration.

Reportedly, FDR's dislike for public school personnel evolved from his opinion that they had not met the needs of the nation's students from low-income families. College preparatory programs were most dominant in the nation's school curricula. The matter of federal funds and accompanying federal control rested heavily on the minds of school leaders. During Roosevelt's time in office and more than two decades later, many public school boards refused the acceptance of federal aid because of their concern of federal intervention. But, at the same time, school districts were in need of monetary support and most all districts agreed to some acceptance of federal funds for vocational education, agricultural programs, special needs programs, payments from federal funds for children of military personnel, and some teacher training programs.

Two of President Roosevelt's official actions gave considerable support to public schools. The rural education program of EEP, previously mentioned, paid for teachers' salaries, which indeed is the major expense of the operating budget of any school. In addition, the federal aid provided to schools for retaining students in school also was a positive provision. Nevertheless, many schools had to close their doors or shorten their school term due to lack of funding from federal aid. The evidence shows clearly that public schools were not sufficiently supported by FDR (Dass, 2014). Also, the literature supports the fact that Roosevelt did not want to support public schools that were failing students.

In addition, Roosevelt held the opinion that public school personnel did not want to make the necessary changes needed to meet student interests and unique needs. He did not want to support the lack of responsiveness needed to make changes that met these needs of students. Of course, federal aid for schools nationally is a major financial consideration. Vocational education in the public schools of the nation was rapidly increasing in costs. Dass' study suggests that the behind-the-scenes works of Roosevelt and Harry Hopkins were responsible for withholding federal aid to education bills and not the more popular contentions of race and religious issues.

Roosevelt's presidential legacy encompasses policies and programs for dealing with the nation's depression, the New Deal and relief, and World War II. Educational programs related to Roosevelt's New Deal policies included the support of public schools in rural areas, job training, the initiation of adult and correspondence courses, vocational courses such as industrial arts and home economics in schools, student aid programs and the vital educational program of the GI Bill, focus on literacy education provisions, adult education programs, preschool nursery activities, and other programs that focused on Roosevelt's New Deal and relief purposes. Productive citizenship, job skills, national defense, government/school relationships, and federal involvement in education all were revealed during Roosevelt's two terms in office.

The evidence would support Roosevelt's concerns for children and youth and their public school education. Without question, Roosevelt's educational views and contributions opened more widely the federal government's involvement in public school policy matters. His criteria for federal aid to education, the GI Bill, and New Deal Programs all contributed to the equalization of education opportunities for the children, youth, and adults in America (Charles, 1982).

HARRY S. TRUMAN

Harry S. Truman could possibly be given "first prize" for having the most viable quotations that present his views on public education. However, the specific contributions to public education for this president are limited. The following seven quotations demonstrate Truman's views on the importance of education in regard to freedom, defense, and personal welfare.

> Without a strong educational system democracy is crippled, knowledge is not only the key to power, it is the citadel of freedom.
>
> Education is our first line of defense. In the conflict of principle and policy which divides the world (today), America's hope, our hope, the hope of the world, is in education.
>
> If peace is to endure, education must establish the morality unity of mankind.
>
> For our day, and our children's day, education must become a continuing adventure in human understanding shared by all.
>
> What may have been sufficient yesterday is not sufficient today. New and terrible responsibilities have been placed on education.

Harry S. Truman (1945–1953)

I think the country is great on account of its small education institutions more than anything else. In institutions such as these the teachers and professors are giving individual attention to each member of the class.

To take full advantage of the increasing possibilities of nature, we must equip ourselves with increasing knowledge.

In spite of the foregoing positive views on education, Truman's inaugural speech of January 29, 1949, had no words regarding public school education apart from a or reference to the importance of a wider and more vigorous application of modern scientific and technical knowledge to greater production, which he presented as key to prosperity and peace. Nevertheless, Truman took specific steps to improve higher educations community education, adult education programs, and public school education—through federal aid supplements—in order to bring the programs of poorer states closer to those of wealthier states.

Although President Truman did not possess a college degree, his report of 1947 on the Commission of Higher Education proposed major changes in higher education by focusing on the present problems of teacher shortages, by giving assurance to the place of higher education in the national efforts to strengthen democracy at home, and by improving the understanding of the nation's neighbors around the world (Truman, 1947). The work of the commission had implications for the support of elementary and secondary education as well. In addition, the work of the commission called for an expansion of adult education and financial support for the first two years of college for all youth that could benefit from such education.

The results of the commission's efforts were revealed in major expansions of junior colleges which evolved into community colleges nationally. Community colleges emerged to become an integral part of a state's educational program. Gutek (1986) points out that "community colleges came to provide continuing education for medical technicians, for industrial training, and for technical skills, to serve as educational, recreational, and social centers for adult learners, and to provide educational and cultural activities and programs for community residents" (264).

Other educational contributions of Truman include such provisions as support for federal aid for public school education and the appointment of the Presidential Committee on Civil Rights that focused on equal rights for black children educationally. Actions by this commission served to increase attention to the unfair treatment of black citizens and led to many historical court cases such as the *Brown v. Board of Education of Topeka* in 1954 that dealt with the issue of segregation in the public schools. In this famous court case, the U.S. Supreme Court ruled that segregated schools were "inherently unequal," and thus violated black rights under the Fourteenth Amendment of the U.S. Constitution.

Even though most individuals recall the memories of Harry Truman for his ending of World War II by using the atomic bomb on two major cities of Japan and the firing of General Douglas MacArthur, his education legacy is noteworthy without question. If our chapter purpose permitted, the listing of some of Truman's humorous quotations could be listed for a smile or two. Perhaps just five such quotations will suffice:

> I never gave anybody hell. I just told them the truth and they thought it was hell.

> You want a friend in Washington? Get a dog.

> If you can't stand the heat, get out of the kitchen.

> I remember when I first came to Washington. For the first six months you wonder how in the hell you even got here. For the next six months you wonder how the hell the rest of them got here.

> The buck stops here.

DWIGHT D. EISENHOWER

Dwight D. Eisenhower (1953–1961)

Dwight D. Eisenhower's education legacy centers primarily on four major happenings involving an historical *Brown v. Board of Education of Topeka* in 1954, Eisenhower's $1.3 billion four-year school construction program, the National Defense Education Act (NDEA), and the court ruling for the integration of schools in Little Rock, Arkansas. In the *Brown v. Topeka* case, the Supreme Court ruled that state law establishing separate schools for black and white schools was unconstitutional. This declaration paved the way for integration nationally. Just how integration was to be carried out was not made clear by the ruling. Thus, this problem has to be confronted during the years that followed. In a follow-up court case, the court merely stated that integration has to be carried out as speedy as possible.

In the four-year school construction program during Eisenhower's presidency, Congress allocated $1.3 billion for school construction. The bill ran into a mountain of controversy. Some persons stated that federal funding was not needed. Fear of additional federal control of state program activities was voiced. In addition, the growing size of the federal budget was expressed by others. Others argued that federal support would lead to greater financial support by the states and their local school districts. There was no doubt, however, that new school construction and repair was badly needed in America's country and city schools. Many schools were outdated in regard to program needs and student safety.

The National Defense Education Act of 1957 was put into place in schools across the nation. The competition between the United States and Russia particularly forced the idea on the public scene that America was falling far behind Russia, Japan, and other foreign nations in regard to students' achievement in the areas of mathematics and science. In addition, foreign languages were being taught in the early school programs of schools internationally and American foreign language programs were not providing satisfactory results.

Upon signing the National Defense Education Act, President Eisenhower stated:

> I have today signed into law H. R. 13247, The National Defense Education Act. This Act which is an emergency undertaking to be terminated after four years, will in that time do much to strengthen our American system of education so that it can meet the broad and increasing demands imposed upon it by considerations of basic national security.... Much remains to be done to bring American education to the levels consistent with the needs of our society. The federal government having done its share, the people of this country, working through their local and state governments and through private agencies, must now redouble their efforts toward this end. (Eisenhower, 1958)

Eisenhower expressed his caring attitude toward children in his January 7, 1959, State of the Union message. In his message for developing quality standards for teachers, Eisenhower stated:

> Consider our schools, operated under the authority of local communities and states. In their capacity and in their quality to conform to no recognizable standards. In some places facilities are ample, in others meager. Pay of teachers ranges between wide limits, from the adequate to the shameful. As would be expected, quality of teaching ranges varies just as widely. But to our teachers we commit the most valuable possessions of the nation and of the family—our children.

Books were published with titles that revealed the inadequacies of education programs in America including Bestor's *Educational Wastelands* in 1953, Rickover's *Education and Freedom* in 1959, and Rafferty's *Suffer, Little Children* in 1962. Each of these publications served to add to the citizen's spirited demands for better and more rigorous student academic programs. The new math programs placed an emphasis on understanding as opposed to memorization and manipulation. Science discovery and applications were emphasized in science. Language labs were installed in special classrooms in most high schools. Four years of math, science, and courses in at least one foreign language were set forth as standards in most every high school program.

Just who is to establish such goals/standards is not made clear in Eisenhower's address. Yet, when he speaks of a national goal and standards, it suggests achievements goals for students and curriculum changes that set forth the subjects and standard teaching procedures that followed later in history called common core.

JOHN F. KENNEDY (JFK)

John F. Kennedy (1961–1963)

Although John F. Kennedy did not serve one full term in office as president, and his inaugural address made no mention of education, his follow-up special messages to Congress on education, speeches on the subject of education, legislative activities relative to education, and views on education as revealed in personal quotations served to influence educational practices in public schools and higher education immeasurably.

Without much question, Kennedy goes into the history books as one of the foremost supporters of public and higher education on record. Kennedy's message to the Congress of the United States sets forth his views of major goals of education in America. In that message, he stated that "education is the keystone in the arch of freedom and progress. Nothing has contributed more to the enlargement of the nation's strength and opportunities than our national system of free, universal elementary and secondary education, coupled with widespread availability of college education."

In our opinion, the aforementioned special message to Congress on education is the most significant, well-presented, thorough, and thought-provoking educational speech ever given by any president before or after the date of January 29, 1963. For that reason, the comprehensive coverage of that speech is summarized in the chapter sections that follow. The major themes of Kennedy's speech are as follows: (1) the necessary roads to reach the important national goals for education, (2) the expansion of opportunities for individuals in higher education, (3) improvement of educational quality, (4) strengthening public elementary and secondary education, (5) vocational and special education, (6) continuing education, and (7) conclusion—public education must be reinforced by national support.

As each major section of Kennedy's message is summarized, give thought to the 1963 messages and recommendations that can be identified as being operational in the nation's 2018 educational programs.

The Expansion of Opportunities for Individuals in Higher Education

In this section on Kennedy's message, he stressed that the welfare and security of the nation require that the investment in financial assistance for college students at both the undergraduate and graduate levels be increased. In order to do so, the following six recommendations were set forth:

(1) Extend the National Defense Education student loan program, liberalize the repayment forgiveness for teachers, raise the ceiling on total appropriations, and eliminate the amounts available to individual institutions.
(2) Authorize a supplementary new program of federal insurance for commercial loans by banks and other institutions to college students for educational purposes.
(3) Establish a new work-study program for needy college students unable to carry too heavy a loan burden, providing up to half the pay for students employed by the colleges in work of educational character.

(4) Increase the number of National Defense Education Act fellowships to be awarded by the Office of Education from 1,500 to 12,000, including summer session awards.
(5) Authorize a thorough survey of the need for scholarships or additional financial assistance to undergraduate students so that any further action needed in this area can be considered in the next Congress.
(6) In addition, include a proposed increase of $835 million to expand the number of fellowships and new teaching grants for graduate study in fiscal 1964.

Expansion and Improvement of Higher Education

Kennedy recommended prompt enactment of a program to provide loans to public and nonprofit private institutions of higher education for construction of academic facilities. This need also applied to public community colleges, higher education libraries, new graduate centers, and the continuation and expansion of modern language area centers at both the public and private institutions of higher learning.

Improvement of Educational Quality

Kenney recommended appropriation budget expansions for the National Science Foundation science and mathematics programs and additional funds for research. In addition, he called for a broadening of the Cooperative Research Act for support of multipurpose educational research. The shortage of highly qualified teachers was noted as a primary inhibitor of progress in such fields as mathematics, science, special education, English, and social studies. Therefore, the National Science Foundation Program for training teachers in these areas required expansion and support, as provided in the 1964 budget recommendations.

Strengthening Public Elementary and Secondary Education

Kennedy expressed concern that low teacher salaries were discouraging talented recruits and retention in the education field. As a recommendation for improving this inhibitor, he recommended a four-year program of $1.5 billion to assist the states in undertaking their plans for improving elementary and secondary education. Increases in teacher starting salaries and salary maximums and special salaries for teachers in disadvantage areas were foremost in his recommendations. In addition, the continuation and increase in National Defense Act programs that included improvements in testing, guidance, and counseling programs were highly recommended.

In addition, funding for school buildings and needed classrooms was set forth as critical.

Vocational and Special Education

President Kennedy's support for the nation's educational programs also placed strong emphasis on vocational/technical education. He viewed the present programs in these areas to be "no longer adequate." The complexities of modern science and industrial technology are in need of training at a much higher level than presently being offered. In view of this crucial need, Kennedy recommended new legislation that would aim to double the number of trained workers. Replacement of the 1946 Vocational Education Act with new grant-in-aid legislation aimed to meet the labor market's current need for trained personnel.

Continued Education

Kennedy's comprehensive views on education nationally included preschool, elementary/secondary, community college, and college and university programs. In addition, continuing education received his attention. Continuous programs for self-improvement were viewed as being essential for meeting the needs of a changing society as well as the needs of an estimated 23 million adults who lacked an eighth-grade education. Therefore, a program that assisted all states in the offering of literacy and basic education for adults was recommended in Kennedy's message. Improvement of library buildings and their facilities also loomed important in Kennedy's report.

Kennedy's Message Conclusion

President Kenney concluded his educational message to Congress by stating the following:

> The program here proposed is reasonable and yet far-reaching. It offers Federal assistance without Federal control. It provides for economic growth, manpower development and progress toward our educational and humanitarian objectives. It encourages the increase of the knowledge, skills, attitudes, and critical intelligence necessary for the preservation of our society. It will help keep America

strong and safe and free. I strongly recommend it to the Congress for high priority action.

When we look back to Kennedy's inaugural address of February 20, 1961, included were educational statements that were projected and set forth in his aforementioned message to Congress. That is, his inaugural address included four major educational needs. One need was to provide funding for public schools, higher education, basic research, and medical training. In addition, he spoke of the need of federal assistance for elementary and secondary school construction and the need to increase teacher salaries. Federal loans to higher education to construct student housing, and scholarships for talented college students were also included in his inaugural remarks.

Kennedy's address called for the appointment of a commission to recommend improvements in vocational education and improvements in college and university buildings and facilities, which later were included in his signed legislative act of higher education passed by Congress in 1963. His speeches at Vanderbilt University and speeches on other occasions carried forth the major educational thrusts of providing a free and equal opportunity for all children and youth; ensuring a quality education for all children and youth; improving the quality of public and higher educational programs; meeting the constructions needs of public schools, colleges, and universities; preparation of well-trained teachers who are well paid; and improving the quality of public and higher education nationally.

LYNDON B. JOHNSON

Two opening entries underscore the primary educational views and contributions of President Lyndon B. Johnson. "At the desk where I sit. I have learned one great truth. The answer for all the problems of the world come to a single word. That word is education." In regard to educational contribution, Johnson assumed the leadership for the passage of approximately sixty educational legislative acts (Siegel, 1983). Additionally, the federal budget for education virtually tripled during his term in office. Johnson viewed such expenditures as an investment rather than an expense.

Upon signing the Elementary and Secondary Education Act of 1965, Johnson commented that "I believe no law I have signed or will ever sign means more to the future of America." He noted that the new education bill (1) "served to bridge the gap between helplessness and hope for more than five million educationally deprived children;" (2) "reduce the terrible time lag in bringing new teaching techniques into the nation's classrooms;" (3) "put

Lyndon B. Johnson (1963–1969)

into the hands of our youth more than 30 million new books, and into many of our schools their first libraries;" (4) "strengthen state and local agencies, which bear the burden and the challenge of better education;" (5) "rekindle revolution of spirit against tyranny of ignorance;" (6) "know that education is the only valid passport from poverty;" and (7) "foster great expectations for what this law will mean for all our young people."

The Elementary and Secondary Education Act represented the federal government's deepest plunge into the operations of local and state education governance. An estimated $200 billion was expended in Title I of the act. Head Start funding for preschool children was given substantial support. Federal funding crept further into support for parochial school children. Johnson favored such programs wholeheartedly. Such funding was based on the rationale that it was to be given to the children and not to the school. It is more than difficult to explain this provision. What educational expenditure, for example, would not ultimately be related as beneficial to the children? Teachers' salaries? Bus transportation? Building repairs? New school libraries? Teacher performance pay?

By 2007, the Elementary and Secondary Act had infused $552 billion into public schools nationally. In addition, Johnson's Head Start Program, bilingual education support, immigrant educational support efforts, work-study awards for college students, student loan programs, and other educational support legislation have virtually changed and improved educational opportunities for thousands of the nation's children, youth, and adults. The program emphasis on the disadvantaged, including students with special needs and/or from under-privileged communities, improved provisions across K–12 public education. Yet, college students and adults were among the benefactors of Johnson's educational programs as well.

If a vote were taken, Lyndon Johnson certainly would rank high as a educational president. If it were not for the unfortunate Vietnam conflict that demanded the attention of President Johnson, other educational improvements in public school and higher education programs would have most likely been implemented. Several of Johnson's following quotations serve to support this supposition:

Liberty without learning is always in peril; learning without liberty is always in vain.

Poverty must not be a bar to learning and learning must offer an escape from poverty.

Let us think of education as the means of developing our greatest abilities, because in each of us there is a private hope and dream which, if fulfilled, can be translated into benefit for everyone and greater strength for our nation.

From our very beginning as a nation, we have felt a fierce commitment the idea of education for everyone. It fixed itself into our democratic creed.

As President of the United States, I believe deeply no law (ESEA) I have signed or will ever sign means more to the future of America.

Education is no problem, it is an opportunity.

In this free land, the minds of our young are our most valuable resource. The classroom teacher is always the steward of that resource. For our prosperous nation and our growing population, no challenge is greater on our horizon than preserving and raising higher the standards of public education.

We have entered an age which education is not just a luxury permitting some men an advantage over others. It has become a necessity without which a person is defenseless in this complex, in industrialized society. We have truly entered the century of the educated man.

Califano, Jr. (2008) summarized Lyndon Baines Johnson's education legacy as follows:

> Lyndon Johnson died . . . in 1973. But his legacy endures. It endures in the children in Head Start programs in hamlets across the nation, in the expanded opportunities for millions of blacks, Hispanics and other minorities. It endures in the scholarships and loans that enable the poorest students to attend the finest universities. . . . The legacy also endures—let us remember—in the unfinished business of our nation's long progressive movement that he pressed so impatiently for us to finish. LBJ knew that the progressive movement could be stalled, but he knew that it must never be stopped. . . . With these acts, President Johnson and Congress wrote a record of hope and opportunity for America.

RICHARD M. NIXON

Richard M. Nixon (1969–1974)

Richard Nixon's legacy is likely to be inhibited by the fact that he resigned the presidency before the end of his second term under the pressure of

Watergate. Nilsson and Bloch (2017), put it this way: "In time, Americans may acknowledge Nixon's mark on history aside from his crimes. But for the troublesome future, his popular legacy will be limited to Watergate and his resignation." "Nixon wanted to be judged by what he accomplished. What he will be remembered for is the nightmare he put the country through in his second term and for his resignation" (Ambrose, 1991, 592). Perhaps Nixon should have practiced what he preached. In one of his quotes, he stated: "Defeat doesn't finish a man, quit does. A man is not finished when he is defeated. He's finished when he quits."

Nevertheless, Nixon had a comprehensive understanding of the importance of education for America's democratic, industrial, and sustainable purposes. His views relative to the many educational provisions are discussed in the following sections on Nixon's educational history. Our focus here is on Richard Nixon's views and contributions to public schools and higher education. The following information is based on a study paper in which Vice-President Nixon discusses education. The study paper was dated September 25, 1960, approximately twelve years before the Watergate scandal.

The 1960 study paper included Nixon's statement that "we are living in a world and at a pitch of crisis that puts an ultimate premium on sheer brainpower-fully developed and unstintingly applied. We dare not waste it; we dare not misapply it; we dare not be satisfied with standards of mediocracy. This is the challenge to American education and we have no time to lose."

The primary points of Nixon's education study report centered on such statements as

- the critical demand for trained acute minds, the threat of communism to the future of education, and the requirements of the time for creative genius;
- the teaching profession and the need to attract the best talent and professional training and the improvement in the art of teaching through research and study;
- the setting of sights for new construction in relation to classroom needs in local school districts and colleges;
- the acceptance and maintenance of standards of excellence;
- the crucial need for all Americans to be skilled in the ways of free citizenship, urgency of increasing teachers' pay, and funds for needed school construction;
- the needed financial support for improving education at the higher levels of colleges and universities;
- the much needed improvement of teacher performance and updated educational materials and equipment;
- the funds needed for continued professional growth of the nation's school teaching personnel;

- the improvement of medical and nursing for attending to student health and welfare;
- the need for federal funding for supporting vocational education in school, college, and university educational programs;
- the need to strengthen the nation's programs of adult education;
- the importance of improving school library facilities in rural city school districts; and
- the important need for establishing a commission on education for the purpose of advising the president, evaluating what needs to be done educationally, and assuring sustained support in the implementation of recommended educational improvements.

Although the foregoing listing is painted with a broad brush, the listing of educational needs, as recommended by Richard Nixon, meets the purposes of this chapter in that the recommendations did indeed reflect his views of the nation's public and higher education needs at the time these were presented.

Nixon expressed other views on educational matters during his vice-presidency under President Eisenhower and later during his time as president. For example, as early as 1954, he stated that the United States should demonstrate, by example, the dream of equality of education, employment, and opportunity.

Nixon expressed his concern over the difference between the performance of public and private schools in America. He noted that although he supported public schools, the difference between the scholastic performance of public and private schools was shocking (1992, 283). He expected students to know the rudiments of a foreign language, be able to know at least a few great works of Western music, and understand the tenets of Christianity, Judaism, Islam, Buddhism, and the world's other great religions such as Marxism-Leninism. Students should know the history of America and something of the history of the world.

Nixon favored higher salaries for teachers but based on performance rather than seniority. In addition, he wanted educational preparation institutions to focus on what to teach as opposed to how to teach. He believed that parental choice was essential but how this factor would be instrumental in promoting educational improvement was not detailed. He pointed to the 1972 Equal Opportunities Act as being in the right direction for meeting the current needs of education. As vice-president, he suggested the passing of the aid to education bill, but he cast the final vote against federal aid for teachers' salaries that cut that provision from the bill.

Nixon's rationale relative to paying teachers' salaries from federal funds is somewhat difficult to report. He definitely stated that he did not want the federal government paying teachers' salaries directly due to the possibility of the federal government gaining control over public school education. Yet, he seemed to favor giving federal money to the states and letting the states make the decision on how the funds were to be expended. Such a procedure, somehow, would obviate the control of the federal government over public school education. The "scheme" appears to be that of providing federal funds for school construction. In turn, money saved on construction can be diverted to payment of higher teacher salaries.

We next give specific attention to Nixon's contributions to education and the extent to which his presidential efforts contributed to the improvement of education in America. It is interesting to note that historians commonly report on Nixon's signing of the Higher Education Act, Title IX, which revolutionized women's involvement in sports. The 1972 Act stated that "no person in the United States, on the basis of sex, shall be excluded from participation in, be denied the benefits of, or be subject to discrimination under any educational program or activity receiving federal financial assistance." Sports programs for girls in public schools nationally expanded throughout the nation. Sports facility construction was extended necessarily, which resulted in major increases in school funding.

One reference (Richard Nixon Foundation, 2017) reported that the Nixon years witnessed the first large-scale efforts to desegregate the nation's public schools. Nixon assigned Vice-President Agnew to lead a task force to determine how to integrate local schools. Considerable progress on the matter of desegregation was evidenced and by September 1970, reportedly, less than 10 percent of black children were attending segregated schools. However, desegregation continued in schools in the North and busing of black students to desegregated schools ultimately was ruled by the court.

Richard Nixon's primary focus during his time in office was on foreign affairs. His efforts on the matter of environmental protection are noteworthy. He signed five notable environmental acts including the Clear Air Act of 1972, the Marine Mammal Act of 1972, the Marine Protection, Research, and Sanctuaries Act of 1973, the Endangered Species Act of 1973, and the Safe Water Act of 1974. Although Richard Nixon's views on education were comprehensive and forward looking, his actual contributions to education, perhaps, are less impressive.

GERALD R. FORD

Gerald Ford was effective in the office of president during his two years and five months of service. Nevertheless, his legacy rests in his signing of the

Gerald R. Ford (1974–1977)

Handicapped Children's Act, now called the Individuals with Disabilities Education Act (IDEA). Ford, himself, had some reservations about the act that provided support services for all handicapped children. His major concern centered on the strain of the bill's monetary resources on the government's total budget. At the time of the signing of the bill on November 29, 1974, Ford commented that "unfortunately, this bill promises more than federal government can deliver, and its good intentions could be thwarted by many unwise provisions it contains."

Ford had other educational contributions that focused on desegregation and providing equal access to education regardless of gender. Many other actions by Ford, outside the specific consideration of education, were especially noteworthy. For example, inflation was reduced by 7.6 percent during his term in office. Employment increased, farming income reached a record high, crime rates decreased, peace was prevalent, and other important improvements were in evidence. Earlier in his political career as congressional representative, he sponsored an educational bill that allowed a credit against the individual income tax for tuition paid for the elementary and secondary education of dependents.

The 1975 Public Law 94–142, Education for all Handicapped Children, is viewed as one of the most comprehensive laws in the history of education in the United States. This legislation has served to bring together various pieces of state and federal legislation making free and appropriate education to all eligible children and youth in America. The law was amended in 1986 to extend coverage to children of a younger age. Later, in 1990, IDEA extended its definitions of "handicap" to "disabilities." Other service improvements are made to IDEA as new provision needs are required.

President Ford left the president's office in 1977 after being defeated by Jimmy Carter. Even after leaving the office, Ford worked with Jimmy Carter to increase the participation of minority students in programs within higher education. Equal rights in education will always be expressed in Gerald Ford's education legacy.

Many people will remember Ford's noticeable "clumsiness" in departing from an airplane or his golf shots that all too often headed for the fairway viewers. In the case of Gerald Ford, it is difficult to think about his legacy without thinking about his wonderful sense of humor. A few examples of his humorous quotations are as follows:

> I would hope that understanding and conciliation are not limited to the 19th hole.
>
> I know that I am getting better at golf because I am hitting fewer spectators.
>
> I am a Ford, not a Lincoln.
>
> Richard Nixon was offered $2 million by Schick to do a television commercial for Gillette.
>
> I watch a lot of baseball on the radio.

DISCUSSION QUESTIONS

1. The topic of federal support of education has been a primary concern throughout the history of America. What is your opinion of federal aid to education at this point and time?
2. Review the education legacies of presidents in chapter 4 and write out one paragraph on one of them as to why he should be among the best education presidents in our history.
3. The Premise: President Nixon was among our best educational presidents in spite of the fact of his forced resignation from office. Take a pro or con position on the premise and set forth your argument to support your position

REFERENCES

Ambrose, S. E. (1991). *Nixon ruin and recovery, 1973–1990*. New York: Simon & Schuster.

Califano, J. A. Jr. (2008, May 19). Seeing is believing: The enduring legacy of Lyndon Johnson. Address given at the Centennial Celebration for President Lyndon Baines Johnson. Kaiser Family Foundation, Washington, DC.

Charles, W. M. (1982, October–November). Franklin Roosevett and equal educational opportunity. *High School Journal*, 66, no. 1: 56.

Couch, C. J. (1989). *Social Processes and Relationships: A formal Approach*. Dix Hills, NY: General Hall Publications.

Dass, P. (2014). Deciphering Franklin D. Roosevelt's educational policies during the Great Depression (1933–1940). An unpublished doctoral dissertation. Scholarly Works @ Georgia State University. Deron Boyles, PhD, Doctoral committee chair.

Eisenhower, D. D. (1958, September 2). Statement by the president upon signing the National Defense Education Act. Online by Gerhard Peters & John T. Wooley. *The American Presidency Project*. From the web: http://www.presidency.ucsb.edu/ws/?pid=11211

Gower, C. W. (1967). The civilization conservation corps and American education: Threat to local control? *History of Education Quarterly*, 7, no. 1: 58–70.

Gutek, G. L. (1986). *Education in the United States: An historical perspective*. Englewood Cliffs, NJ: Prentice Hall.

Kennedy, J. F. (1963, February 20). Special message to Congress on education. Online by Gerhard Peters and John T. Wooley. *The American Presidency Project*. http://www.presidency.ucsb.edu/ws/pid=8433

Nilsson, J., & Bloch, P. (2017, August 9). Nixon's resignation and the legacy of a flawed president. *The Saturday Evening Post*. Indianapolis, IN: The Saturday Evening Post Society.

Nixon, R. (1992). *Seize the moment*. New York: Simon & Schuster.

Richard Nixon Foundation. (2017, August 4). Nixon's record on civil rights. From the web: https://www.nixonfoundation.org/2017/08/nixons-record-civil-rights-2/.

Siegel, P. (1983). *Lyndon Baines, Johnson and Education*. ERIC Number: ED 279601.

Truslow, P. (2013, November 6). Accomplishments of Herbert Hoover. *Chrome Network*.

Truman, H. S. (1947, December 15). Statement by the President making public a report of the commission on higher education. *The American Presidency Project Online*. From the web: http://www.presidency.ucsb.edu/ws/?pid=31906

Chapter 5

Education Legacies of U.S. Presidents 1977–2020

The New Millennium Era of Terrorism, Immigration, and "Making America Great Again"

Primary chapter goal: To present views and primary educational contributions of the nation's presidents during the end of the twenty-first century.

Selected historical happenings that influenced this era: Iran hostage crisis; fall of the Berlin Wall; Persian Gulf War; JFK assassination; Clinton impeachment and pardon; election turmoil; September 11, 2001; terrorism; the New Millennium; Bush and no new taxes; 2017 Trump election; North Korea nuclear threats; concerns on weather changes; immigration controversies; educational voucher controversy; and Hurricanes Harvey and Irma.

JIMMY CARTER

Perhaps Carter's most impressive quotation on education was his statement that "education is our most important national investment. . . . Our ability to advance both economically and technologically, our country's entire intellectual and cultural life depends on the success of our great educational enterprise" (Carter, 1979). He expressed the opinion that the primary responsibility for education should rest with those states, localities, and private institutions that have made the nation's education the best in the world. Nevertheless, he believed that the federal government needed to have a full-time commitment to education at every level of government: federal, state, and local.

Carter exhibited early signs for the support of public education even before being inaugurated as president of the United States in 1977. As Georgia's governor, he voiced the position that the days of discrimination were over. His focus on public education featured his intentions to support vocational education and to equalize other educational practices such as state financial

Jimmy Carter (1977–1981)

support and reducing class size throughout the state of Georgia (Wikipedia, 2017). He also assumed leadership in establishing the state's free kindergarten, extended programs for handicapped students, and expanded educational programs for prison inmates.

Carter favored private education and at one point told the audience to not ever let anyone be misled into criticizing private education. Nevertheless, Carter contended that the federal government should pay a higher percentage of the cost of public education. Carter's educational program would create a separate department of education, increase vocational and career opportunities, increase the funding support for the education of handicapped students, focus on strengthening the financial support of colleges and universities, and do more educationally for the elderly (Carter, 1976).

Carter is credited for the establishment of the first department of education at the federal level in 1979. Yet, the history of a federal department of education somewhat parallels that of a roller coaster, up and down, high and low. Kosar (2015) points out that Andrew Johnson launched the first department of education in 1867 even though Congress, just one year later, reduced it to an office not represented in the cabinet. It was soon relegated to a bureau function within the U.S. Department of the Interior. Some years later in 1939, the bureau was placed within another agency and renamed the Office of Education. Fourteen years later, the Federal Security Agency was upgraded to cabinet-level status as the Department of Health, Education, and Welfare (Wikipedia, 2017).

Although President Carter signed the Department of Education Organization Act on October 17, 1979, it did not begin operating until May 4, 1980, some seven months later. The department's mission centered on bringing the nation's education challenges and federal government's role to the forefront of domestic policy discussions.

President Carter listed six specific responsibilities for the department: (1) to increase the nation's attention to education; (2) to make federal education programs more accountable; (3) to streamline administration of aid-to-education programs; (4) to save tax dollars by eliminating bureaucratic layers and reducing personnel; (5) to make federal education programs more responsive; and (6) to ensure that local communities retain control of their schools and education programs (Carter, 1979). Without question, Carter's strong belief in the separation of church and state was the foundation of his education legacy. This strong commitment did tend to upset religious groups, which had more interest in gaining a role in matters of politics, including the politics of education.

In 1980, the Republican Party platform called for the elimination of the Department of Education. President Reagan called for the elimination of the department as a cabinet post, but this did not take place. Later, Robert Dole, a presidential candidate, pushed for the elimination of the department. The department continued under George W. Bush, and in 2007, a bill signed by Bush designated the ED Headquarters building as the Lyndon B. Johnson Department of Education Building. Once again, on February 7, 2017, a bill to abolish the department was submitted that called for the abolishment of the department on December 31, 2018.

RONALD REAGAN

We begin the educational legacy discussion of Ronald Reagan by asking you to take the following pretest. The true and false questions posed are intended to engage your interest in Reagan's views and specific contributions regarding education especially during his two presidential terms from 1981 to 1989. Check each of the ten statements either true or false, but refrain from just guessing the correct response. If you are not quite certain of the answer to a question, just move on to the next entry.

Ronald Reagan (1981–1989)

PRE-CHAPTER QUIZ

True or False

1 President Reagan's first legislative action upon his entry into the presidency was to sign a bill that eliminated the Department of Education, one of his oft-stated campaign promises. ____True or ____False
2 Although it is true that one of Reagan's quotes stated that "but there are advantages to being elected president. The day after I was elected I had my high school grades classified Top Secret," he called for an increase in standardized testing in schools. ____True or ____False
3 President Reagan was strong in the belief that teachers should be paid on the basis of merit. ____True or ____False
4 President Reagan called for a constitutional amendment that mandated prayer in schools. ____True or ____False
5 Reagan stated that "America's schools don't need new spending programs; they need tougher standards, more homework, merit pay for teachers, discipline, and parent back in charge." ____True or ____False

6 In his First Inaugural Address in 1989, the last one-fourth of President Reagan's message focused on the importance and immediate needs of improvements in public education. ____True or ____False
7 Reagan was of the belief that enough had been done with the emphasis on math and science in the public school program. He proposed that the curriculum focus on an understanding of the world around them (students). ____True or ____False
8 Reagan favored the passage of tuition tax credit for parents who wanted their children to attend private or religiously affiliated schools. ____True or ____False
9 Regan has been quoted as saying, "But the most important thing we can do is to reaffirm that the control of our schools belongs to the States, local communities and, most of all to the parents and teachers." ____True or ____False
10 Reagan favored vouchers for public funds for public and private schools. ____True or ____False
11 Reagan contended that teachers should be paid on the basis of their merit. ____True or ____False
12 In his First Inaugural Address to Congress, Reagan stated that "all of us need to be reminded that the Federal Government did not create the States, the States created the Federal Government." ____True or ____False

ANSWER KEY

True or False

1. The answer to statement #1 is False. Although Reagan called for the abolishment of the Department of Education during his candidacy, he changed his mind after being elected. Upon being elected, he took no actions toward the department's elimination. In fact, he worked with his secretary, Terrel Bell, to place an emphasis on promoting excellence in all matters of education. One emphasis "pushed" by Reagan was the implementation of standardized testing. In fact, improvements in test scores on the part of schools and school districts, after the enforcement of standardized testing, did not occur.
2. The answer to statement #2 is True. The implementation of standardizing testing of students' academic performance was a key approach to accountability in the opinion of Reagan. In the long run, however, more testing did not result in the improvement of student learning. School labels became prominent during this era. Labels such as "high-performing school" and "low-performing school" were given commonly

by state departments of education. In some instances, school principals were dismissed when their school did not show improvement on required standardized test scores.

3. The answer to statement #3 is True. *Grolier Encyclopedia* (2000) noted that Reagan did support mandatory prayer in the public schools, although the idea was never accepted by Congress.
4. The answer to statement #4 is True. In fact (Cannon, 1991) notes that Reagan did indeed call for a constitutional amendment to restore prayer in schools. Historians view such actions on Reagan's part as being more of a "political statement" to give comfort to the religious right.
5. The answer to statement #5 is True. Strauss (2011a) notes that Reagan spoke at the Eleventh Annual Conservative Political Action Conference dinner in March 1984 and stated that "America's schools don't need new spending programs; they need tougher standards, more homework, merit pay for teachers, discipline, and parents back in charge." Reagan expressed his belief that education was the primary responsibility of the states on numerous occasions. In his First Inaugural Address to Congress, however, he commented on the powers granted to the federal government and those reserved to the states. His specific statement in the address deserves some attention. Reagan stated that "all of us need to be reminded that the Federal Government did not create the States; the States created the Federal Government." Is this a what-came-first question? What came first, the chicken or the egg?
6. The answer to statement #6 is False. In fact, Reagan's First Inaugural Address never mentioned the word *education*. At one time in the address, Reagan noted that it was his intention to curb the size and influence of the federal government and to demand recognition of the distinction between the powers granted to the federal government and those reserved to the states or to the people (as set forth in the Tenth Amendment to the U.S. Constitution). Of course, education was one of the responsibilities so reserved.
7. The answer to statement #7 is False. In fact, Reagan was highly in favor of improving math and science education in the public schools. In his 1983 State of the Union Message to Congress, he stated, "In 1983 we seek four major educational goals: (1) a quality education initiative to encourage a substantial upgrading of math and science instruction through block grants to the States." His three other goals focused on (2) the establishment of education savings accounts that would give middle and lower-income families an incentive to save for their children's college education, (3) passage of tuition tax credits for parents who want to send their children to private or religiously affiliated schools, and (4) a constitutional amendment to permit voluntary school prayer.

8. The answer to statement #8 is True. As noted in the answer to number 7, Reagan did indeed favor giving tuition tax credits to families that wanted to send their children to schools other than public schools. This intention, however, was never accepted by Congress.
9. The answer to statement #9 is True. Reagan's support of local control of education was underscored in his 1988 State of the Union Message to Congress. Specifically, he stated, "But the most important thing we can do is to reaffirm that control of our schools belongs to the States, local communities and, most of all, to the parents and teachers." Bachman (2011) told of Reagan's statement that he had never believed in federal control of the schools. He believed that the majority of parents could do the best job of thinking what was best for their child's education and how to provide them with the proper values. That is what Reagan meant by local control: letting the fifty states chart their own course on education. That is, he believed that a good school was best addressed as close to the parents as possible.
10. The answer to statement #10 is True. Reagan publicly stated that he favored financial support for public schools as well as private schools.
11. The answer to statement #11 is True. Although Reagan believed in higher salaries for teachers, he also was of the belief that teachers' salary should be based on merit.
12. The answer to statement #12 is True. In his First Inaugural Address to Congress, Reagan did state that "all of us need to keep in mind that the Federal Government did not create the States, the States created the Federal Government." We conducted an unscientific study of ten people and asked them the foregoing question. One hundred percent of them believed that the federal government did indeed create the states. What is your thinking on this question? Our thinking on this matter is that the selected representatives in the Congress of the United States are made up of people of the fifty states. Therefore, the states did and do create the federal government.

Reagan's Education Legacy in Summary

President Reagan's education legacy is summarized under the headings of the following actions:

(1) Strong critic of the Department of Education as a presidential candidate but continued and supported the department after its inauguration
(2) Favored school vouchers for public funds for tuition for private and/or religious schools

(3) Supported mandatory prayer in the public schools but would settle for an amendment to the U.S. Constitution to restore voluntary prayer in schools, but this was not to happen
(4) Strongly "pushed" for the teaching of national pride in schools with a student understanding of freedom
(5) Advocated for the nation's commitment to excellence in school programs evidenced by major improvements in student academic performance. Not just more and more money for education, rather a commitment to quality
(6) Proposal to target assistance to low- and middle-income families for paying for public school taxes and private school tuition
(7) The establishment of education savings accounts as college incentives for encouraging substantial upgrading of math and science education, establishing of educational savings accounts for needy families, passing of tuition credits, and a constitutional amendment to permit voluntary school prayer

GEORGE H. W. BUSH

President George H. W. Bush mentioned education only once in his Inaugural Address on January 20, 1989. Nevertheless, he did talk about what was great in America and the fact that it could be made even better. The importance of an educated citizenry was inferred throughout his references to the needs for high moral principles, helping young mothers, helping the homeless, solving the crimes on the streets, and other things that America must do to fulfill its purposes of a democracy and freedom of people.

The following quotation by George Herbert Walker Bush is unique among the nation's presidents. Other presidents certainly have held this belief, but none were known to express this thought so vividly in public. During a debate with Governor Michael Dukakis, Bush expressed the fact that he wanted to be the education president, because he wanted to see us do better. He noted that "we're putting more money per child into education, and we are not performing as we should. . . . And I would like to urge the school superintendents and others around the country to stand up now and keep us moving on a path toward real excellence."

On other occasions, Bush stated, "Think about every problem, every challenge, we face. The solution starts with education." He viewed education as the key to opportunity and as a ticket out of poverty. Several writers have reported President George H. W. Bush's actual educational views and specific contributions. For example, in one speech, Bush promised that by the year 2000, the U.S. students would be first in the world in math and science achievement. In reality, by the year 2000, the U.S. students ranked eighteenth in mathematics and fourteenth in science.

George H. W. Bush (1989–1993)

In a following debate on October 5, 1992, Bush set forth several general statements relative to parental choice. He talked about reinventing American schools by developing a new generation of American schools by turning the land into a nation of students and, in the process, turning himself into a computer genius. The specifics of these statements are not clear.

In his 1990 State of the Union Address to Congress, however, Bush did set forth America's six education goals: (1) By the year 2000, every child must start school ready to learn; (2) the United States must increase the high school graduation rate to no less than 90%; (3) make sure our schools' diplomas mean something. In critical subjects at the fourth, eighth, and twelfth grades, we must assess our students' performance; (4) by the year 2000, U.S. students must be first in the world in math and science achievement; (5) every American adult must be a skilled, literate worker, and citizen; and

(6) Every school must offer the kind of disciplined environment that makes it possible for our kids to learn.

> Bush: I'd be delighted to, because you can't do it the old way. You can' do it with the school bureaucracy controlling everything. We have a new program that is now in 1,700 communities across the country. It's called America 2000k. It literally says to the communities: Reinvent the schools, not just the bricks and mortar but the curriculum and everything else. Think anew. We have a concept called the New American School Corporation, where we're doing exactly that. So I believe that we've got to get the power in the hands of the teachers, not the teacher union. So our American 2000 program also says this: It says let's give parents the choice of public, private, or religious school. And it works. It works in Milwaukee. Competition does that. So we've got to innovate through school choice. (October 15, 1991)

George H. W. Bush was mentioned only twice in the listing of best education presidents conducted by the website "Learning Masters," a nonprofit company that focused on education (Strauss, 2011b). However, he was mentioned along with eight other presidents who could contend for "best education president." His actual education accomplishments, however, do not measure up to his being named in this category. On one occasion during a presidential debate, he was asked about being an educational president. On one occasion during a debate with Governor Michael Dukakis, he was asked about being an educational president. Bush spoke candidly in his following response to the question: "I want to be the education President, because I want to see us do better. . . . And I would like to urge the school superintendents and the others around the country to stand up now and keep us moving forward on a path toward excellence" (1988, September 25).

WILLIAM J. CLINTON (BILL)

President Clinton did not mention the word *education* in his First Inaugural Address on January 20, 1993. However, he did express his hopes for education in his Second Inaugural Address four years later. In that address, he stated:

> In this new land, education will be every citizen's most prized possession. Our schools will have the highest standards in the world, igniting the spark of possibility in the eyes of every girl and every boy. And the doors of higher education will be open to all. The knowledge and power of the Information Age will be within reach not just of the few, but of every classroom, every library, every child. Parents and children will have time not only to work, but to read and play together. And the plans they make at their kitchen table will be those of a better home, a better job, the certain chance to go to college.

William J. Clinton (1993–2001)

Kathleen Koch (1999) set forth Clinton's education plan as follows:

The way in which federal aid is invested for schools must be changed. Accountability measures must be implemented that require states and school districts to turn around or close failing schools. Annual report cards must be given to parents on how each school, school district, and state schools as a whole are performing. No child should have to go to a failing school. Social promotion is to be ended by making sure that students have the support for meeting higher standards. Summer school and after-school programs are to be extended with additional funding. Subject matter and skills tests for new teachers are to be administered. School safety measures, including anti-drug programs, will be required. What works, and we know what works, will be supported by federal funding.

The history of Clinton's presidency does not reveal substantial evidence of positive follow-up on the several specific aspects of the foregoing educational plan. Clinton encountered other matters that served to overshadow his presidential contributions, including his major troubles relative to impeachment in office. However, Clinton's major educational legislation, the Improving America's Schools Act, was foremost in his contributions to education. The America's Schools Act reauthorized the Elementary and Secondary Education Act of 1965 for five years. The law authorized $11 billion in fiscal 1995 for most federal K–12 educational programs and enacted program changes that were viewed as most significant since the Elementary and Secondary Education Act was first passed in 1965. The foregoing act was a major part of Clinton's efforts to reform education.

When speaking of the new economy, Clinton stated that "in the new economy, education is everything." He seemed to favor prayer in schools as well. One of his quotations that serves to support this contention was as follows: "It appears that some school officials, teachers and parents have assumed that religious expression of any type is inappropriate or forbidden altogether in public schools; however, nothing in the First Amendment converts our public schools into religion-free zones."

During Clinton's presidency, education did receive additional funding. Primary and secondary education increased from an average of $8.5 billion before his presidency to $11.1 billion during his terms in office. This funding, of course, supported the America's Schools Act that also increased funding for higher education. Student Pell grants were increased, and other student assistance for students in higher education was increased as well. Student loan programs were improved under the Student Loan Reform Act that included direct federal loans to students. Educational technology was expanded with addition funding that rose from $27 million in 1994 to $769 million by the year 2000, a phenomenal increase in federal support.

Bill Clinton was impeached by the House of Representatives on December 19, 1998, on charges of lying under oath to a federal jury and obstruction of justice. He was acquitted of both articles of impeachment by the Senate on February 12, 1999.

GEORGE W. BUSH

In one listing of the nation's best education presidents, George W. Bush was ranked third. Only Abraham Lincoln and Dwight D. Eisenhower ranked higher than him. The historical record tends to support Bush's ranking in this regard. His *NCLB* legislation, signed in 2001, set forth major steps ahead for improving education in the United States.

President Bush's concern for public education was shown in his early political career as the Governor of Texas. According Karl Rore (2010, 111), Bush made the improvement of reading in Texas' schools a top priority. As president, Bush was cognizant of education as being a state and local

George W. Bush (2001–2009)

responsibility, but, at the same time, he believed that the federal government could serve to encourage change and improvement in education at the local level. His early focus on reading received positive support from educators and parents in local communities.

In 2006, in his State of the Union Address, he announced the American Competitive Initiative that centered on three primary objectives: (1) to double the federal commitment to the most critical basic research programs in the physical sciences; (2) to make permanent the research and development tax credit to encourage increased private sector initiative in technology; and (3) to encourage students to take more math and science in order to improve the performance in these subject fields. Bush proposed extensive programs to train thousands of high school teachers to take the lead in the teaching of advanced placement courses and train thousands of other teachers to help other students who need special help in learning math and science.

Reading improvement was a topic of primary interest for Bush throughout his terms in office as Governor of Texas from 1995 to 2000. As president, he enthusiastically endorsed the teaching of reading through the use of phonics. Bush's Reading First Program distributed $412 million to several states to help schools and districts improve children's reading achievement using what was then termed "the scientifically proven methods of instruction." According to Ivins (2000), in 1998, as governor, Bush made forty-seven speeches on education, which included an emphasis on reading. At one time, he stated, "Now is the time to teach all our children to read and renew the promise of America's public schools." He underscored the belief that failure to teach all children to read was discriminatory and, like all other forms of discrimination, it should be ended.

When speaking of his *Reading First* program, Bush referred to reading as a national emergency. Five billion dollars was proposed to fund the diagnosis of reading problems, teacher training, and intervention programs directed toward disadvantaged children to help them learn to read. The goal was to help every child be able to read by the end of grade three. Ninety million dollars was to be allocated for teacher training in research-based reading instruction for kindergarten and first-grade teachers. Another $90 million was to be used for intervention funds, after-school programs, tutoring, and summer school programs that focused on reading improvement.

Bush had no room for failure educationally. However, he expected student achievement in return for federal support; federal dollars would no longer follow failure. Although he expressed his support of local control of education, accountability for achievement results was expected; schools were to be held accountable for learning results. He contended that a simple question was to be asked, what are the results? Are children learning? Rewards were proposed for positive learning results. If not, the money would go to the parents who would make a different choice of schools to attend.

No Child Left Behind

The (NCLB) Act of 2002 had major impacts on school programs nationally and faced both praise and criticism. As reported by the Educational Research Center (2015), the NCLB Act updated the Elementary and Secondary Education Act and significantly increased the federal role in public education. A primary feature of the act was that it focused on accountability of schools for student performance results. As a result of its impact on the curricular programs in schools, teaching content and methods, and increased standardized testing, the law became increasingly controversial.

Although the act had the "good" intentions of helping all students improve their academic performance, its special focus was on the improvement of learning for English-language learners, special education students, and children of poverty or minority status. The federal control factor was in what might be termed a "catch-22" position, either comply with the requirements of the law or no federal Title 1 funds would be available to the school program.

Schools and school districts had to submit a progress plan that centered on an adequate annual progress statement identified as the AYP: adequate yearly progress. As the NCLB Act stated: (1) A school that did not meet their AYP two years in a row had to allow students to transfer to another district school; (2) A school that did not meet their AYP three years in a row was required to establish a program of free tutoring; (3) Schools that continued to miss their AYP faced the probability of being shut down or facing other intervention strategies determined by the state; and (4) Schools that did not achieve their AYP goals faced the loss of federal dollars that could be used for other "worthy" education purposes.

As would be expected, the NCLB Act faced considerable criticism. Interventions and alternatives, among other factors, were matters of concern. As a result, the requirements of the law were changed, dropped, ignored, or reprogrammed and ignored. The law ultimately fell into the hands of President Obama whose dealing with the law is discussed in the following section.

BARACK OBAMA

One cannot help but be impressed by President Obama's statement about the importance of teachers in the overall picture of a child's education. Spina (2011) calls our attention to Obama's State of the Nation Address when he said, "Let's also remember that after parents, the biggest impact on a child's success comes from the man or woman at the front of the classroom. In South Korea, teachers are known as 'nation builders'. Here in America, it's time we treated the people who educate our children with the same level of respect." Obama went on to encourage all young persons to consider becoming a teacher. In doing so, the individual could make a difference in the life of a child and underscored the fact that the nation needs such talents.

There is no other more comprehensive source for President Obama's educational views and contributions than the *On the Issues* summary titled "Barack Obama on Education," as last updated on October 12, 2016. Virtually every act of this president in the area of education is summarized in that article. Although information relative to the various legislative actions of

Barack Obama (2009–2017)

Obama are discussed in other publications, no other source that we researched is as complete and informative as this *On the Issues* content. Information in this article is based on such resources as President Obama's State of the Union addresses, Obama's presidential debates, Obama's interviews, Obama's speeches, and various articles authored by many individuals.

We set the scene of Obama's education legacy by presenting several of his quotations on the subject. Of all the presidents studied in the preparation of this book, the educational statements of President Obama certainly are the most extensive. Although we have made every effort to remain neutral relative to reporting the educational views and contributions of the forty-four national presidents, we note that one reference (Strauss, 2011) would most likely rank Obama as being tied for last among the nine presidents listed as "best" education presidents.

In a second listing of best education presidents (Roberts, 2009), Barack Obama was not even listed among the top-twelve education presidents of the United States. Historical evidence would suggest a much higher rating for this president. One web reference listed education presidents in the following order: (1) Dwight Eisenhower, (2) Abe Lincoln, (3) George W. Bush,

(4) Franklin D. Roosevelt, (5) Gerald Ford, (6) Lyndon Johnson, (7) Richard Nixon, (8) Andrew Johnson, (9) Woodrow Wilson, (10) Harry Truman, (11) Benjamin Harrison, and (12) Bill Clinton (TeachHUB.com). After reading the educational history of the forty-four national presidents presented in this book, how might you list the best educational presidents who have served in the presidency?

Selected Educational Quotations of Barack Obama

Several educational quotations of Barack Obama were selected to illustrate his views on education and its importance:

> Our higher education system is only one of the things that makes America exceptional. There is no place else that has the assets we do when it comes to higher education. People from all over the world inspire to come here and study here. And that is a good thing.

> It is not enough to train today's workforce. We also must prepare tomorrow's workforce by guaranteeing every child access to a world-class education.

> Every young person in America deserves a world-class education. We've got an obligation to give it to them.

> We have an obligation to be investing in our students and our schools. We must make sure that people who have the grades, the desire and the will, but not the money, can still get the best education possible.

> We still live in a country where too many are priced out of the education they need. It's not fair to them, and it's not smart for our future. That is why I am sending this Congress a bold new plan to lower the cost of community college—to zero.

> [Starting] 5 years ago, 'Race to the Top' has helped raise expectations and performance. Some of this change is hard. But it's working. The problem is we're still not reaching enough kids, and we're not reaching them in time. This has to change.

> The agenda starts with education. A highly-educated and skilled workforce will be the key not only to individual opportunity, but to the overall success of our country as well.

> Our public education system is the key to opportunity for millions of children. . . . It needs to be the best in the world. Of particular concern is the growing achievement gap between the middle and low-income students, which has continued to expand despite some overall nation national achievement gains.

> You know, sometimes I'll go to an eighth-grade graduation and there's all that pomp and circumstances and gowns and flowers. And, then I think to myself, it's just eighth grade. To really compete, they need to graduate high school, and then they need to graduate college, and they probably need a graduate degree.

An eighth-grade education doesn't cut it today. Let's give them a handshake and tell them to get their butts back in the library.

In the following section, we describe several educational contributions of President Obama as revealed in his State of the Union addresses, presidential debates, interviews, related education articles, speeches, and other personal conversations and campaign messages. The entries are presented objectively in that no judgments are made relative to their positive or negative reception by the people or to education's improvement as a result of their implementation. In some cases, the entry is simply a position that Obama took on an educational matter or one that he strongly believed was of major importance for improving education nationally.

Race to the Top—Obama believed that a high-quality education in the early life of a child was of paramount importance for the child's success. He wanted a prekindergarten program for every child at age four. As one might expect, the program was controversial for several reasons. One reason, of course, was the involvement of the federal government in public education at the state level.

Obama's *Race to the Top* program, that was intended to encourage creative ideas and activities for improving education, was funded with $4.5 billion, viewed as a modest amount of money. States competed for the funds. Monetary awards were given to only eleven states and the District of Columbia. Criticism of the program was rampant after rewards were announced. The major contention was that the creative awards were given on a political basis as opposed to the quality of the ideas for reform submitted by the various states.

The Hiring of More Teachers

In one Obama-Romney debate in 2012, the topic of hiring more teachers and class size was brought to the floor. Obama contended that his administration had been working with the governors of forty-six states on education and progress had been seen. Apparently, Romney stated that class size did not make a difference and Obama replied, "You said that class sizes don't make a difference. But I tell you, that teachers will tell you it does make a difference." This is a case of neither candidate really knowing the results of existing research on class size. However, both candidates were partially correct. In a meta-analysis of research on the topic, it was found that classes with fifteen students or less were associated with improved academic performance. Effects were strongest in the early grades and among low-income students (Glass & Smith, 1979). In all fairness, it is noted the aforementioned research has been criticized reportedly on the basis of its flawed research methodology.

A Plea for Every American to Graduate from High School and Beyond

In his State of the Union Address in 2009, Obama asked every American citizen to complete additional education after graduating from high school, at least one year. Not doing so was to quit on oneself and one's country. In Obama's opinion, the United States should have the highest proportion of college graduates in the world. Specifically, Obama stated, "If you commit to serving your community and your country, we will make sure that you can afford a college education."

A Hit on NCLB

In a speech given in Flint, Michigan, Obama took exception with George W. Bush's NCLB legislation by saying that it alienated teachers and school administrators, and although well intended, it did not serve the purpose of inspiring school personnel. Obama wanted to take a new and different direction that centered on new policies that resulted in new knowledge and skills for creating jobs and opportunities for dealing with personnel needs of the future. He wanted to fix the failures of NCLB by investing several million dollars in a program of quality, affordable, early childhood education for every child in America.

Getting the Parents Involved in Their Child's Education

Barack Obama was of the opinion that getting parents involved in their child's education was of paramount importance. While the government has an obligation in funding education, parents have to do their job of initiating an educational environment in the home. Fun and games, TV, and video games had to give way to learning activities that are planned and enforced in the home for supporting the child's school success and future success in other job pursuits and higher education.

The Hiring of Thousands of New Teachers in High-Need Areas of the Nation

Obama campaigned with intentions to fully support the necessary funding for Head Start and the expansion of preschool programs in low-economic and high-need communities. Specifically, he proposed the addition of 25,000 new teaching personnel for high-need rural and urban school communities. In addition, he campaigned to support deserving students' college education by way of loan programs. Such loans would be controlled outside commercial banks so as to protect students against high-interest loan rates.

Common Core

Common core represented a giant step into the state control of educational programming. Formalized curricula based on the expected knowledge-base of K–12 students and methodological teaching were at the "core" of the Common Core State Standards. Although the program faced national criticism due to its control requirements, all states except Texas, Virginia, Alaska, Nebraska, Indiana, and Minnesota adopted the program. The 2009 presidential debates gave considerable attention to Common Core educational requirements with the states' rights contenders leading the way toward repealing the law.

Other Obama Educational Programs and Presidential Contentions

Although many educational programs and activities of Barack Obama were criticized for political reasons and fears of extended federal control, his educational legacy, as mentioned previously, was most impressive. Without question, Obama gave considerable attention to public education. His record in this regard is historically extensive. In closing Obama's education legacy, we list several other program ideas and/or educational activities in which he was clearly involved. These program contentions are listed as follows:

- Treating teaching like the profession that it is: If we invest in our teachers, our children will succeed.
- Free college education for any student that maintains a B-average in high school.
- Double charter schools but no vouchers to be given.
- Support community college learning centers.
- Additional funding support for community colleges.
- Expand Pell grants for millions of students.
- Establish community career centers in all community colleges.
- A college degree, not only a high school education, is the goal for education today.
- We should forgive student loans for students who perform public service.
- Favored refundable $4000 tax credit for community college tuition.
- Pay for the college of education for those persons who commit to a teaching career.
- Lower the cost of a community college to zero dollars.
- Make mathematics and science education a national priority.
- Increase after-school and summer programs with expected parental support.
- Make math and science policy a national priority.

- Ten billion dollars to guarantee early childhood education for all.
- Get parents much more involved in the education of their children.
- Establish a program for school construction on a national basis.

DONALD J. TRUMP
(Time Will Tell)

President Donald Trump's time in office had just passed 273 days, approximately three-fourths of one year, at the time of this writing. Thus, writing about a legacy in his case is certainly premature. His inaugural address of January 21, 2017, made no mention of education except to say that Americans want great schools for their children. Nevertheless, it is possible to identify Trump's views on many educational policies and related issues, and this section will identify and briefly discuss these views. What is said by an individual during his or her candidacy for a political office and what is said and done upon being elected, as we have seen historically, are sometimes quite different.

Donald J. Trump (2017–present)

We have been able to gather enough evidence on certain educational views to report them here as the expressed educational views of Donald Trump. At the outset, we identify several of his educational views that were set forth some years prior to his assuming the office of president. In turn, his views after becoming president will be addressed. Actual legislative actions on education have yet to be determined.

School Choice

Trump's position on *school choice* was expressed many years ago in his article "The America We Deserve" (2000, July 2). The message set forth by Trump was that the teachers' unions' views on school choice, as being threatening to the continuation of public education, were that the union needed to retain the lion's share of the educational market or that their survival was problematic. Trump noted that the courts had broken up one large commercial company that had 90 percent of the market and it survived. His contention was that school choice is the best option since it constitutes a competitive system and competition fosters improved education.

In the same publication mentioned earlier (Trump, 2000), Trump set forth three additional educational perspectives: (1) Schools are not safe and kids are not learning. Student dropout rates were escalating and the "dumbing down" of the public school curriculum was a major problem. Not enough was being asked of teachers and students. Attention to the important topic of citizenship was void leaving students without the qualities of good-study habits and readiness for additional learning. (2) Current attitudes of educators, that we need to handle students with kid gloves, are faulty. Exactness, as opposed to estimation, is what is needed to foster needed quality. (3) Competition is necessary to break down the stalemate of educational improvement. Public education must be able to produce a more competitive product than it is doing at the present time.

In several other early publications and speeches, before assuming the office of president, Trump expressed other educational views as related to school vouchers, charter schools, student loans, common core, the Department of Education, comprehensive education, and others. Such views were set forth in a variety of addresses, interviews, publications, and conferences. In a brief article in *USA Today* (2017), it was reported that President Trump, while in office, had directed the Education Secretary Betsy DeVos to prioritize science and technology education and to spend at least $200 million annually on competitive grants. Trump had noted that more than half of U.S. high schools do not teach computer programming. The importance of this information is vested in large part by the fact that this was an early sign that Trump did have a direct interest in public education.

School Choice as a Civil Rights Issue

On February 28, 2017, Trump announced that he was calling on members of both parties that would fund school choice for disadvantaged youth, including millions of African-American and Latino children. Trump emphasized his belief that these families should be able to choose the type of school that is right for their children. This contention opened a wide door, one that has been most controversial historically. Trump identified that such choices included public, private, charter, magnet, religious, and home schooling.

In an earlier article by Parker and Gabriel (2016), Trump voiced the following intention: "As president, I will establish the national goal of providing school choice to every American child living in poverty. . . . If we can put a man on the moon, dig out the Panama Canal, and win two world wars, then I have no doubt that we as a nation can provide school choice to every disadvantaged child in America." In a *CBS News* article by Julia Boccagno (2016), Trump once again pronounced his deep concern for school choice: "As your president, I will be the biggest cheerleader for school choice you've ever seen" (1).

Opposition to Common Core

As early as 2015, Donald Trump referred to *common core* as a disaster and noted that it was not only a waste of money but invaded the authority of the states to determine the education of students. At the time of this pronouncement, he emphasized the fact that he was not cutting services but might cut the Department of Education. He was adamant about the fact that education was a local responsibility and that it should not be decided by a bunch of Washington, D.C., bureaucrats. At this time, he voiced the view that the Department of Education could be cut down substantially. In a radio interview with Hugh Hewitt (2015), Trump made it clear that education should be local and that the federal government's role was not to control it but to support it.

In an article by Saul (2016), it was noted that views of common core tend to carry a bit of misunderstanding. He contended that common core standards were adopted by the states and that recently enacted law prohibited federal government from mandating educational standards that the states must adopt. He concluded by insisting that the Department of Education at the federal level had no authority for common core provisions. Stratford (2016) tends to support this contention. As he stated in an article in 2016, some of Trump's pitches, like scrapping common core, are clearly outside the bounds of what a president can actually do. Yet, such claims as Stratford's statement seem to be receiving major challenges each and every day in the politics of modern America.

Views on Education as Revealed in Trump's Planned Budget: As Reported by the *Washington Post*

Perhaps a relatively recent article by Brown, Strauss, and Douglas-Gabriel (2017, May 17) provides the best available source of Trump's views regarding education. In their article, "Trump's First Full Education Budget: Deep Cuts to Public School Programs in Pursuit of School Choice," the authors describe the "probable" results of the Trump's educational budget on educational programs and practices.

For example, the authors note that funding for college work-study program would be cut in half; public service loan forgiveness would end; and other dollars for mental health, advanced course work, and other services would be substantially reduced when plans for carter schools and voucher systems were adopted. Cuts in other ongoing educational programs seem imminent. Although still unofficial, best information suggests that education department budget cuts would reach $9.2 billion. Some programs, such as special education and Title 1 funding, would remain unchanged.

Brandon L. Wright (2016) gives us additional insights into President Trump's views on education in his article "President Donald Trump Quotes about Education." Besides the previous views on school choice, common core, and the U.S. Department of Education, Trump's views on other educational matters are mentioned here. Several of his educational statements were set forth while campaigning for the presidency and before.

On the control of education, Trump stated:

> Keep education local!
>
> There is no failed policy more in need of urgent change than our government-run education monopoly.

On citizenship education, Trump stated:

> Public education was never meant to only teach the three R's, history and science. It was also meant to teach citizenship.

On the matter of student loans, Trump stated:

> A four-year degree today can be expensive enough to create six-figure debt. We can't forgive these loans, but we should take steps to help students. . . . These loans should be viewed as an investment in America's future.

On comprehensive education, Trump stated:

> Comprehensive education dissolves the lines between knowing too much and knowing too little on a variety of subjects—subjects that are necessary for success.

One significant program change centers on a new grant program named Furthering Options for Children to Unlock Success (FOCUS). School districts would agree to allow students to choose which public school they attend. Federal, state, and local dollars would follow the student. Other "options" set forth by the Trump administration, such as school zoning, Title 1 dollars to follow the student, and the loan forgiveness program, are viewed as quid pro quo options that venture close to voucher-type arrangements.

Of interest is the current situation relating to the Department of Education. As previously noted, earlier Trump suggested that he might cut the department. His proposed budget, on the other hand, seeks an additional $158 million for salaries and expenses in the education department up 7 percent. Yet, according to the Brown, Strauss, and Douglas-Gabriel report, the workforce in the department would be decreased by approximately 150 positions. Early statements regarding Trump's education budget suggest cuts in funding for the purpose of promoting funds for choice. Yet, time will tell. As noted, at the time of this writing, Trump's education budget was just a proposal. Congress, of course, will have much to say about this important matter. Changes based on bias, whim, politics, and lack of knowledge will always fail. What is needed is a strong new effort for educational research that provides a knowledge basis for leading improvement.

DISCUSSION QUESTIONS

1. Assume the position of school superintendent of the Lafayette School District. You are asked to speak at the annual state superintendents' conference on the topic of school choice. Draft two or three paragraphs that reveal the main points of your address to this group of administrators.
2. In his first inaugural address, Ronald Reagan stated that "the Federal Government did not create the States, the States created the Federal Government." How is Reagan's statement to be interpreted? Just what was he trying to get across to the citizenry?
3. Bill Clinton once stated that "in the new economy, education is everything." Explain the meaning of his statement. Be specific in your written response.
4. Rate Barack Obama's education legacy on a scale of 1 for low and 10 for high. Then, write one or two paragraphs to support your ranking.
5. By the time that you read this chapter, President Trump will have completed additional months in the office of president. On the basis of what you have read about or witnessed his educational views and contributions at this point in time, write an additional one or two paragraphs that provide additional information about his educational legacy.

SELECTED HISTORICAL EVENT IN THIS ERA

A Failed Assassination

One of the negative happenings during this era was the near-assassination of President Ronald Reagan. Although most everyone recalls something of this happening, hearing the story from the ex-president himself is enlightening in itself. Reagan's book, *The Reagan Diaries,* edited by Douglas Brinkley, and published by HarperCollins (Reagan, 2007), tells the following story of the event as remembered by Reagan.

Monday, March 30, 1981

Left the hotel at the usual side entrance and headed for the car—suddenly there was a burst of gun fire from the left. S. S. Agent pushed me onto the floor of the car and jumped on top of me. I felt a blow in my upper back that was unbelievably painful. I was sure that he'd broken my ribs and had punctured a lung. The car took off. I sat up on the edge of the seat almost paralyzed by pain. Then I began coughing up blood which made both of us think—yes I had broken a rib and it had punctured a lung. He switched orders from W. H. to Geo. Wash. U. Hosp.

. . . I walked into the emergency room and was hoisted onto a cart where I was stripped of my clothes. It was then we learned that I'd been shot and had a bullet in my lung . . . Getting shot hurts. Still my fear was growing because no matter how hard I tried to breathe it seemed I was getting less and less air. . . . I focused on that tiled ceiling and prayed. . . . I opened my eyes to find Nancy there. . . . All the kids arrived and the hours ran together in a blur during which I was operated on. I know it's going to be a long recovery but there has been such an outpouring of love from all over. (12)

REFERENCES

Boccagno, J. (2016, September 20). Where Donald Trump stands on education. *CBS News*. CBS Interactive Inc.

Brown, E., Strauss, V., & Douglas-Gabriel, D. (2017, May 17). Trump's first full education budget: Deep cuts to public school programs in pursuit of school choice. *Washington Post*. From the web: https://www.washingtonpost.com/local/education/trumps-first-full-education-budget-deep-cuts-to-public-school-programs-in-pursuit-of-school-choice.

Bush, G. H. W. (1988, September 25). Debate with Michael Dukakis. Transcript. Miller Center, University of Virginia. From the web: https://millercenter.org/the-presidency/presidential-speeches/september-25-1988-debate-michael-dukakis

Bush, G. W. (1998, December 31). George W. Bush on accountability. Supports vouchers, including private or religious schools. From the web: www.csmonitor.com/durable.1997/12/05/us/us.1.html

Cannon, L. (1991, July 2). The role of a lifetime. As listed in *On the Issues*, Ronald Reagan on Education, Presidents of the U.S., 1881–1989.

Carter, J. (1976, July 15). "Our Nation's Past and Future": Address Accepting the Presidential Nomination at the Democratic National Convention in New York City. *The American Presidency Project*. From the web: http://www.presidency.ucsb.edu/ws/index.php?pid=25953&st=&st1=

Carter, J. (1979, February 13). Department of Education message to Congress. Transmitting Proposed Legislation. Online to Proposed Legislation Online by George Peters and John T. Wooley *The American Presidency Project*. From the web: http://www.presidency.ucsb.edu/ws/?pid=31906

Glass, G. V., & Smith, M. L. (1979). Meta-analysis research on class size and achievement. *Education Evaluation and Policy Analysis*, vol. 1, no. 1, 2–16.

Golier Encyclopedia on line. (2000, December 25). The presidency. As listed in *On the Issues*, Ronald Reagan on Education. Presidents of the U.S., 1981–1989.

Hewitt, H. (2015, February 25). Hugh Hewitt radio interview on 2016 presidential hopefuls.

Higgons, Lori. (2017, September 25). President Trump and Invanka Trump unveil 200 million dollar coding education grant. *Detroit Free Press*. From the web: https://www.usatoday.com/story/tech/news/2017/09/25/pres-trump-ivanka-trump-unveil-200-million-coding-education-grant/701566001/

Koch, K. (1999, May 19). Clinton releases education plan. CNN.

Kosar K. R. (2015). Kill the Department of Education? It's been done. *Politico*.

Parker, A. & Gabriel, T. (2016, September 8). Donald Trump releases education proposal, promoting school choice. *New York Times*. From the web: https://www.nytimes.com/2016/09/09/us/politics/donald-trump-education

Reagan. R. (2007). *The Reagan Diaries*. Edited by Douglas Brinkley. New York, NY: HarperCollins Publishers.

Roberts, W. B. C. (2009). Top 12 presidents to influence education. *Teach-HUB. K–12 Teachers Alliance*. From the web: http://www.teachhub.com/top-12-presidents-influence-education.

Rove, K. (2010). *Courage and Consequence: My Life as a conservative in the Fight.* New York: Thresh Id Editions.

Saul, S. (2016, November 21). Where Donald Trump stands on school choice, student debt and common core. *New York Times.*

Siegel, P. J. (1983). Lyndon Baines Johnson and education. ERIC. Non-Journal. ED.gov.ies. Institute on Education Sciences.

Spina. (2011, February 17). Teachers under attack (p. 80). As listed in *On the Issues*, Ronald Reagan on Education. Presidents of the U.S., 1981–1989.

Stratford, M. (2016, November 9). What Donald Trump's stunning win means to education. Morning Education. *Politico.*

Strauss, V. (2011a, February 6). Ronald Reagan's impact on education today. The Answer Sheet: A School Guide for Parents. *Washington Post.*

Strauss, V. (2011b, November 21). Who was the best education president? *Washington Post.*

Strauss, V. (2015, December 17). Don't blame George W. Bush for what President Obama did to public schools. *Washington Post.*

Trump, D. (2000, July 2). *The America we deserve* (p. 83). In *On the Issues*, Donald Trump on Education. 2016 Republican Nominee for President.

Wikipedia. (2017, August 15). *United States Department of Education.* From the web: https://en.wikipedia.org/wiki/United_States_Department_of_Education

Wright, B. L. (2016, November 23). President Donald Trump quotes about education. *Flypaper* (blog). Thomas B. Ford Institute. From the web: https://edexcellence.net/articles/president-donald-trump-quotes-about-education

Appendix

Special Exercise

SELECTION OF TOP-TEN EDUCATION PRESIDENTS

Directions: You have had the experience of learning about the primary educational views and contributions of each individual who has served as president of the United States. Many publications have been written on the personal and presidential histories of the nation's presidents, including surveys and individual opinions of the "best" and the "worst" presidents who have served the nation.

In the following activity, however, we ask you to select the ten best educational presidents. Although you most likely will have to base your opinion on the information gained in reading the five chapters of this book, you might have other bases for making your choices. Try to keep in mind that you are not being asked to pick the best president who has served our country; rather, you are selecting the ten *best education presidents* based on their expressed educational views and their accomplishments in education during their work in public office and during their tenure in office as president of the United States.

We list the names of the forty-four presidents of the United States and ask you to select the twelve best educational presidents. Then, list each of these twelve presidents in rank order. Of course, your first choice will be #1 and last choice will be #12.

Use your personal opinion in making the choices. When and if you find some difficulty in making a decision, take a moment to review the legacies of the president that you have in mind in the appropriate section of the book.

Special Exercise

List of All U. S. Presidents in Order of Service   RANK only the Best Twelve <u>Education</u> Presidents: 1 first, 12 last

George Washington (1789–1797)   ———
John Adams (1797–1801)   ———
Thomas Jefferson (1801–1805)   ———
James Madison (1809–1817)   ———
James Monroe (1817–1825)   ———
John Quincy Adams (1825-1829)   ———
Andrew Jackson (1829–1837)   ———
Martin Van Buren (1837–1841)   ———
William Henry Harrison (1841–1841)   ———
John Tyler (1841–1845)   ———
James K. Polk (1845–1849)   ———
Zachary Taylor (1849–1850)   ———
Millard Fillmore (1850–1853)   ———
Franklin Pierce (1853–1857)   ———
James Buchanan (1857–1861)   ———
Abraham Lincoln (1861–1865)   ———
Andrew Johnson (1865–1869)   ———
Ulysses S. Grant (1869–1875)   ———
Rutherford B. Hayes (1877–1881)   ———
James A. Garfield (1881–1881)   ———
Chester A. Arthur (1881–1885)   ———
Grover Cleveland (1885–1889) & (1893–1897) ———
Benjamin Harrison (1889–1893)   ———
William McKinley (1897–1901)   ———
Theodore Roosevelt (1901–1909)   ———
William H. Taft (1909–1913)   ———
Woodrow Wilson (1913–1921)   ———
Warren G. Harding (1921–1923)   ———
Calvin Coolidge (1923–1929)   ———
Herbert Hoover (1929–1933)   ———
Franklin D. Roosevelt (1933–1945)   ———
Harry S. Truman (1945–1953)   ———
Dwight D. Eisenhower (1953–1961)   ———
John F. Kennedy (1961–1963)   ———
Lyndon B. Johnson (1963–1969)   ———
Richard M. Nixon (1969–1974)   ———
Gerald R. Ford (1974–1977)   ———
Jimmy Carter (1977–1981)   ———

Ronald Reagan (1981–1989)   _____

George H. W. Bush (1989–1993)   _____

Bill Clinton (1993–2001)   _____

George W. Bush (2001–2009)   _____

Barack Obama (2009–2017)   _____

Donald J. Trump (2017–)   _____

Now check your listing with that of the author's ranking and the consensus of opinions set forth in the TeachHub.Com list. Is there evidence of agreement between your listing and the two listings that follow? Don't worry, I just hope that you enjoyed doing the exercise.

AUTHOR'S TOP 12 BEST EDUCATION PRESIDENTS	TEACHHUB.COM'S TOP 12 BEST EDUCATION PRESIDENTS
1. Lyndon B. Johnson	1. Dwight D. Eisenhower
2. George Washington	2. Abraham Lincoln
3. Thomas Jefferson	3. George W. Bush
4. John F. Kennedy	4. Franklin D. Roosevelt
5. Dwight Eisenhower	5. Gerald Ford
6. James Madison	6. Lyndon B. Johnson
7. George W. Bush	7. Richard Nixon
8. Herbert Hoover	8. Andrew Johnson
9. Ronald Reagan	9. Woodrow Wilson
10. Jimmy Carter	10. Harry Truman
11. Gerald Ford	11. Benjamin Harrison
12. Franklin D. Roosevelt	12. Bill Clinton

Glossary

Burthens—An archaic form of the word "burden."
Civic literacy—The knowledge of how to actively participate and initiate changes in the community and greater society.
Common school—A public elementary school commonly including both elementary and secondary grades.
Continental Congress—A convention of delegates from the first thirteen colonies, which became the governing body of the colonies from 1774 until 1789 when George Washington became the first president of the United States.
Divine right—The belief that the monarch's authority comes directly from God rather than from the consent of the people.
Egalitarianism—The doctrine that all people are equal and that all people deserve equal rights and opportunities.
Era of enlightenment—An intellectual and philosophical movement that dominated thinking and the world of ideas during the eighteenth century. Rationalism came to advance ideas relative to liberty, tolerance, scientific methods, and knowing.
Grammar schools—Another term for elementary schools. In the United States, a school for young children, and in Great Britain, a school for children over age eleven.
Legacy—Something handed down from one generation to the next. A U.S. president leaves a legacy of beliefs, reputation, views, contributions, and achievements of outcomes while serving his or her term(s) in office.
Liberal education—A system or course of education suitable for the cultivation of a free people. It is based on the liberal arts and intended to bring about improvement, discipline, and free development of the mind and spirit.
Popular government—A government that is controlled by the people by election of executives and legislators.

Popular information system—A preferred and organized system for the collection, organization, storage, and communication of information. Popular information is that communication most preferred by persons to receive.
Public domain—The state of belonging or being available to the public as a whole and therefore not subject to copyright.
Public school—A school supported by public funds for the education of children of a community or district that constitutes a part of a system of free public education commonly including primary and secondary schools.
Rationalism—A belief or theory that opinions and behaviors should be based on objectivity, reason, and certainty of knowledge.
Reconstruction—The period of 1865–1877 following the Civil War, during which time the states of the Confederacy were controlled by the federal government and local legislation, including the granting of new rights for African-Americans, was introduced.
Republic—A country that is governed by elected representatives and by elected leaders. The supreme power rests in the body of citizens entitled to vote by representatives elected or chosen indirectly or by them.
Separatism—The advocacy or practice of separation a certain group of people from a larger body on the basis of ethnicity, religion, or gender.
Signal prosperity—A detectable physical quantity or impulse by which messages or information can be transmitted; a sign or state of being that portrays success and/or good fortune.
Unfettered start—Being free to exercise one's behaviors without being bound by shackles or chains.
Women's suffrage—Most commonly directed to the passage of women's right to vote and to stand for electoral office.

About the Author

Dr. M. Scott Norton has served as a secondary school teacher of mathematics, coordinator of curriculum for the Lincoln, Nebraska School District, assistant superintendent for instruction, and superintendent of schools in Salina, Kansas, before joining the University of Nebraska as professor and Vice-Chair of the Department of Educational Administration and Supervision. Later he served as professor and Chair of the Department of Educational Administration and Policy Studies at Arizona State University, where he is currently professor emeritus.

His primary graduate research and instruction areas include curriculum and supervision, teaching methods, governance policy, instructional leadership, educational leadership, human resources administration, the assistant school principalship, research methods, organizational development, and competency-based administration. He has published widely in national journals in such areas as teaching/instructional methods, curriculum development, organizational climate, instructional leadership, gifted student programs, student retention and others.

Dr. Norton has received several state and national awards honoring his services and contributions to the field of educational administration from such organization as the American Association of School Administrators, the University Council for Educational Administration, the Arizona Administrators Association, the Arizona Educational Research Association, Arizona State University College of Education Dean's Award for excellence in service to the field, President of the ASU College of Education Faculty Association, and the distinguished service award from the Arizona Information Service. He presently is serving as a member of the ASU Emeritus College Council.

Dr. Norton's state and national leadership positions have included service as Executive Director of the Nebraska Association of School Administrators, a member of the Board of Directors for the Nebraska Congress of Parents and Teachers, President of the Nebraska Council of Teachers of Mathematics, President of the Arizona School Administrators Higher Education Division, member of the Arizona School Administrators Board of Directors, Staff Associate of the University Council for Educational Administrators, Treasurer of the University Council for School Administrators, Nebraska State Representative for the National Association of Secondary School Principals, member of the Board of Editors for the American Association of School Public Relations, and presently a governance council member for the Emeritus College of Arizona State University.

www.ingramcontent.com/pod-product-compliance
Lightning Source LLC
Chambersburg PA
CBHW021846220426
43663CB00005B/418